The Origin of Rāga

An attempt has been made to trace out the most popular and common terms *rāga*, its origin, techniques and also the course of its development from the Vedic period to this modern age of science. It also narrates *rāga* in actual forms and its development through ancient and medieval times and as it is practised and performed by musicians of the present times. The style of expression is easy to understand and didactic.

with 8 illustrations

The Origin of Rāga

A CONCISE HISTORY OF THE EVOLUTION, GROWTH AND THE TREATMENT
OF RĀGA FROM THE AGE OF BHARATAMUNI TO BHATKHANDE

S. Bandyopadhyaya

Munshiram Manoharlal
Publishers Pvt. Ltd.

ISBN 978–81–215–0261–0

Third edition 2007

Published by Munshiram Manoharlal Publishers Pvt. Ltd.,
Post Box 5715, 54 Rani Jhansi Road, New Delhi 110 055.

Dedicated

to

Pt. Vadi Lall Shiva Ram Sharma

Sangeetacharya

One of the best disciples of

Pt. V. N. Bhatkhande

Contents

List of Illustrations, *ix*

Exordium, *xi*

Foreword to the First Edition, *xiii*

Abstract from the Preface of the First Edition, *xv*

1 Conception of Music, *1*

2 The Origin of Rāga, *22*

3 The Treatment of Rāga, *49*

Appendix, *71*

Bibliography, *78*

Index, *81*

List of Illustrations

1. Basanta Rāga. Rajput Miniature (Bikaner), about AD 1800.

2. Bhairava Rāga. Rajput Miniature, 19th century.

3. Hindola Rāga. Rajput Miniature, 19th century.

4. Megha Rāga. Rajput Miniature (Mewar), about AD 1650.

5. Madhumadhavi Rāgini. Rajput Miniature (Amber), 18th century.

6. Kamod Rāgini. Deccan, 18th century.

7. Megha Malhar Rāga. Rajput Miniature (Amber), AD 1709.

8. Sri Rāga. Rajput Miniature (Amber), AD 1709.

Exordium

It is a pleasure to present the second revised and enlarged edition of this book to all lovers of music, who are in quest of a reliable text book on the history of the evolution, growth and treatment of the particular subject, namely, the Rāga. The first impression of this little book was made available in 1946 and in a very short time all the copies were sold. But due to circumstances it was not possible to have its second edition till now. Very much regretted for the delay.

All informations relating to 'Rāga' are stated in this work in different chapters, to quench the thirst of knowledge even of those, who know nothing about the system of *Rāga*. Bibliography is added to this edition. It is hoped, therefore, that this edition may serve as before, the purpose of all connoisseurs of Indian music.

Before I conclude, I must express my thanks to Messrs Munshiram Manoharlal Publishers Pvt. Ltd., New Delhi, for bringing out this edition.

Shripada Bandyopadhyaya

'SHRIDHAM'
33, Shivaji Park,
Shahdara, Delhi-32.
June 15, 1977.

Foreword

I have great pleasure in introducing to the students of music and the music-minded public this very interesting treatise on the *Origin of Rāga* by Mr. Shripada Bandyopadhyaya, Sangeet Visharad of the Marris College of Hindusthani Music.

The Art of music and dancing has now adequately impressed the public with their benevolent influence on the mind and body, so that an urgent demand has been created for books on the subject. This fulfills its object admirably as regards the subject treated in it. It is the result of a deep and critical study of the available modern and ancient literature on 'rāga' and their origin, on the part of the author, who is himself very well equipped with the knowledge of theory, and practice of music and has had nearly ten years' experience of the work of educating people in music.

It is no wonder that he has made his mark in the field of music, a product, as he is, of the leading institution of music, namely, The All India Marris College of Hindusthani Music, Lucknow. He has now published two other interesting books, namely, *Sitar Marg* a text book on the art of Sitar playing and *The Music of India* besides a little pamphlet containing devotional songs to music, all of which have engaged the attention of the public.

'The Origin of Rāga, is divided into three chapters followed by an appendix. The first two chapters deal with the age of progress of the idea of the 'rāga' and actual forms through which it has gone through during the ancient and medieval times while the third is devoted to the explanation of the forms of the 'rāga' as they are practised and performed at present. It is thus a short historical sketch of our music, and written, as it is, in an easy style of expression, it has become a very handy and useful book of general knowledge of Indian Music.

I am sure that *The Origin of Rāga* will be appreciated by the public and make the efforts of the author successful.

Rajabhaiya Poonchhwale, Sangeetacharya, Principal, Madhava Sangeet Mahavidyalaya, Gwalior; Member of the Senate, Bhatkhande University of Indian Music, Lucknow.

Gwalior,
5th March, 1946.

Preface

The tendency of almost all modern civilised citizens of this country towards Fine Arts and specially to music is very encouraging. The authorities of the different Boards of Education and of many other Universities have included music as a subject in the course of studies along with other subjects. Hence a dearth of good books on the various topics on the theory of the present day music is generally felt by almost every student, lovers of music and casual readers.

The present work, is such as treats the particular subject, namely the '*rāga*,' its origin, growth and also the treatment into minute details. A brief account of which had already been published in '*Nād*,' a musical journal of the Bhatkhande University of Indian Music, Lucknow; in 1941, which was not only approved but also highly admired by Dr. S. N. Ratanjankar, who advised the author to compile a separate book on the subject for the benefit of all advanced students of music.

I can hardly express my obligations to a personality like him, who, inspite of being in the midst of multifarious activities, has very kindly gone through the manuscripts of this book to make it systematic and easy for the students and casual readers of Indian music.

This book has been written purposely for the advanced students and lovers of music on the whole theory of '*Rāga*.' If it proves its usefulness among the students community nothing will give me more satisfaction.

Shripada Bandyopadhyaya

Delhi,
April 14, 1946.

Conception of Music

'Nād'—the eternal sound, one of the five elements of the natural phenomenon, gave birth to the music of the orient and the oxident. Hence, the term music is used all over the world for the three fold arts, namely, the vocal music, instrumental music and also the art of dancing. *viz:*

"गीतं वाद्यं तथा नृत्यं त्रयं संगीतमुच्यते"

The origin of music, therefore, seems to have begun from the primitive stage of mankind—the cave man, with his clan, to convey the idea of their emotions to others. It is the internal flow of some emotions, thoughts and feelings of all human beings irrespective of their nationality, caste and creed. That is, the music is the universal language of the emotions of all artistic souls of all times and places. Although the music of the various nations of different times and places varies according to the taste and likings of the people, but the fact cannot be denied that the effect of music on layman, is almost alike.

India is compact and self contained nation and the inhabitants of this sub-continent had not to work hard because of munificence of her natural sources, unlike others, from the very early age, perhaps even before from the dawn of civilisation of the rest of the world, they cultivated fine arts. Hence in India the people of the Vedic age, were always after the realisation of the truth, and were seekers of the mysteries of nature and were also admirers of natural beauties. Consequently they never failed to express their numerous urges which they usually received from the various sources of nature, called by the Aryans as *'Prakriti,'* mainly through music.

It is stated in the Hindu mythology that the various aspects of life and learnings are associated with different sages. It is natural, therefore, that the mythologists might have ascribed the origin of the art of music to some certain sage according to their belief. It is the conjecture of the Indians that Brahma is the creator of this universe, naturally the origin of music is direct from him. He imparted this heavenly art to Shiva—the god of destruction, who, delivered it to Saraswati—the goddess of knowledge of all arts and literature and she taught it to the heavenly musicians and dancers, namely the 'gandharvas,' 'Kinnaras' and the 'apsarās' respectively. These divinities are supposed to have handed over this art to the great sages like Nārada, Hanumān, Bhārat and many others, who were sent to this world as it were, to divulge it to the mortal beings of this earth.

Indians, particularly the Hindus, belief that salvation can even be obtained through the practice of music, that is why, it is said that to be a great musician, a man must live retired from the world like an ascetic.

This opinion is undoubtedly influenced by a consideration of the lines of the ancient saints and is not perhaps without some truth. This is a fact that some of the greatest artists used to retire to their favourite spots in the woods from where they used to get inspirations. The aid the painter derives from them is evident. It is not only the painter and the poet, however, that befriend such delightful places, the genious of music likewise inhabits there and in a special manner patronises her votaries there. This opinion was also common with the ancient Greeks, as it will appear from the passage quoted from Plato by Dr. Burney. 'The grasshoppers sing all summer without food, like those men, who, dedicating themselves to music, forget the common concerns of life.'

The Music of the Vedic and Paurānic age

In course of time when language developed to some degree of intelligibility proper use of music began to be restricted only to the worship of the Supreme Being. This was the stage, generally known as the music of the *Vedic-Age*. The hymns of the 'Ṛg' and 'Sām' Veda are the earliest examples, we have of words set to music. It is acknowledged by the great scholars of the west that Chanting of the Vedas had been prevalent in India even before 2400 BC and remained so till the first century of the Christian era.

Sanskrit—the high flown language of those days was the only medium of education. All instructions were imparted orally by the masters to their disciples. The 'Ṛg' and 'Sām' Vedic verses as also of the Black Yajurveda are compositions of Sanskrit words with Vedic accents (notes) known as the '*Udātya*' '*Anudātya*' and '*Svārita*.' These accents were considered to be the musical notes of the Vedic and Paurānic age. Their actual position and value were not discussed any-where in any of the Vedic literature, so these accents were lost in the days of Pāṇini—the great grammarian of the Vedic literature.

The ancient Greeks, like Indians, had also their music confined only to four notes. The early Greek lyre had four strings and was confined to four notes. (vide Herbert Spencer's *Origin and Function of Music*). Pāṇini, however, defines the Vedic accents as under:

"उदात्तश्चानुदात्तश्च स्वरितश्च स्वरास्त्रयः" ।
उच्चैरुदात्तो नीचैरनुदात्तः समाहारः स्वरितः ॥

viz. Udātya raised, Anudātya—following accent and Svārita—not raised. He in his 'siksha' has compared the said three well known Vedic accents with the seven current notes of his own time as stated below:

उदात्तौ निषाद गान्धारौ, अनुदात्तौ ऋषभ धैवतौ ।
स्वरित प्रभवाह्येते षड्ज मध्यम पञ्चमाः ॥

He means to say that the current notes of his time namely, 'nishāda and gāndhara,' 'rishāva and dhai-vāta,' and 'sadja-madhayama, pancama' were equiva-lent to 'udātya' 'anudātya' and 'svārita' respectively. It may be noted here that fourteen kinds of poetical metres known as chhanda were also used in chanting the Veda.

Reference regarding the music of the Vedic age can be gathered from Chhandogya and Bruhadāranyaka Upanishada 600 BC, Rāmāyana 500 BC, Mahābhā-rata 300 BC. The actual form of the music of the past is now untraceable, as the Vedas, Samhitās, Brahmanas, Aranyaka, Upanishada, Purāṇ, Upa-purāṇ and Mahā Kāvyas contain no explanation regarding the actual form and system of music of that time. Still it is a

fact, that the music both vocal and instrumental and
also dance were in flourishing condition in those
days, but their principles, systems and also the style
of rendering were unknown even to the scholars of
the medieval age.

The Vedic literature provides a wide range of
musical instruments—that were current in those days.
The instruments of percussion were represented by
the 'dundubhi,' 'bhumidundubhi,' 'adambara' and
'vanaspati.' Stringed instruments were represented by
'kanara veena,' 'karkari' and 'veena.' There were
also a number of wind instruments such as, 'turava,'
'nadi' 'bakura.'

In due course of time seven forms of musical compositions seem to have developed as amply evident
from the ancient text books, which also trace the
music of India to this scale, the notes of which were
known as 'Ārchika'—single note, 'gāthika'—double
note, 'sāmika' of triple note,' 'svarāntar' of quadruple
note, 'shādava' of sextuple note and finally' 'sam-
purana' of the seven notes which were in vogue in
the ancient music of India. *viz:*

आर्चिको गाथिकश्चैव सामिकश्च स्वरान्तरः ।
औडवं षाडवश्चैव सम्पूर्णश्चेति सप्तमः ।   (बृहद्देशी पृ० १७)

History is the weak spot in Indian literature and
specially in that of music. It is in fact not existant.
The lack of historical sense is so characteristic that
the very chronological order of events in connection
with the art and science of music is darkened by the
shadow of this defect. Whatever information is available now-a-days is only through few Sanskrit works
by the various authors of different times and places.

Ancient Schools of Indian Music

It has been traditionally held and also supported by the majority of the scholars of music that there were six main schools or systems, termed by those masters as 'mata' in ancient India. They are known as under: 1. Brahma Mata, 2. Shiva Mata, 3. Nārad Mata, 4. Hanumān Mata, 5. Bhārat Mata, 6. Kaḷi Nath Mata. Some scholars say that the schools founded by 'Brahama,' 'Shiva' and 'Nārada' were the three main systems of Indian music of the past, whereas the others acknowledge that the systems expounded by 'Hanumān,' 'Bhārata' and 'Kaḷinath' were current in those days and the rest considered the following as the leading schools of the by gone age *viz.* Bhārat, Kaḷi Nath and Shiva. There still exist some difference of opinion in this respect due to the absence of definite data either in the form of written records or in that of musical compositions. The work by 'Brahma' and 'Hanumān' are not traceable. Hence, nothing can be said regarding those two schools. Topics of the remaining schools are given below.

Bhārat Mata

The earliest important work, in which the theory of Indian music, particularly the art of dancing is discussed at length, and was explained into minute details by Bharat, the author of 'Natya Shastra,' is considered to be the founder of the present system of music. Some historians assign it to the first century AD, while others to a later period either to the fourth or to the sixth century. It is evident from the text that the music, which was current at his time (first century to the sixth centuries AD), was based on twenty two 'shrutee' (microtonel intervals of sound), seven

sharp 'sudha' and two flat 'vikrita'—(Antara Gāndhara and Kakali Nishada) notes 'svara,' two scales
'grāma' namely, the Sadja and Madhyama, and
lastly twenty one 'moorchana.' Bharat then classifies,
under the two scales 'grama'—the 'sadja' and 'madhyama' eighteen 'jati' in all, for example.

स्वराश्च श्रुतयो ग्रामो मूर्च्छना: स्थान संयुता: ।
स्थानं साधारणे चैव जातयोऽष्टादशैव च ॥

Bharat classifies the above mentioned eighteen jatis
under two scales 'grama' putting seven of them in 'sadja
grama' and the remaining eleven in 'madhyama
grama.' The following verses shall give an idea of the
jatis properly:

Jatis derived from 'sadja-grama':

स्वर साधारण गतास्तिस्रो ज्ञेयास्तु जातय:
मध्यमा पञ्चमी चैव षड्जमध्या तथैव च
स्रासामङ्गानि विज्ञेया: षड्जमध्यम पञ्चमा:
यथास्वं दुर्बलतरा व्यक्ता सा पञ्चमी तथा
षड्जर्षभी धंवती च नैषादी च तथा परा
षड्जोदीच्यवती षड्जकैशिकी षड्जमध्यमा
षड्ज ग्रामाश्रया ह्येते विज्ञया: सप्त जातय:

Jatis obtained from 'madhya-grama':

स्रत ऊर्ध्वं प्रवक्ष्यामि मध्यमग्राम संश्रया:
गान्धारी रक्तगान्धारी गान्धारोदीच्यवा तथा
मध्यमोदीच्य वा चैवं मध्यमा पञ्चमी तथा
गान्धार पञ्चमीचान्ध्री नन्दयन्ती तथापरा
कर्मारवी कैशिकी च ज्ञेयास्त्वेकादशापरा: ।

(नाट्य शास्त्र)

It is now almost impossible to form any idea of jati
that were current in his time, as Bharat did not

locate the actual position of the notes both sharp and
flat, Shruti and also the scales 'grama.' Inspite of the
statement given therein, the subject shall remain
undiscovered, so long as the actual intervals of which
the two scales 'gramas' were composed are not traceable. It is certain that the jatis were a particular type
of ancient music which was current till the seventh
century AD, and that was prior to singing of the Rāga
of the later age.

The system expounded by Bharat seems to have
been known to the sage Duṭila, mention of whom is
very frequently made by Bharat in his work, as one
of his sons *(putra)*, whom he had taught the theory
and practice of music. Duṭila was earlier than the
saint Matanga, who also quotes him in his work
'brihaḍesi.' There is a mass of evidence to show that
the work was largely used for study by later authors
on music. Duṭila is also cited as an authority by
Abhinava Gupta in his well-known commentary
'Abhinava Bhārati' on the 'Nātya Shāstra.'

Duṭila also accepts the same eighteen jatis that
were enumerated by Bharat in his work, 'Nātya
Shāstra.' The following verses quoted from 'duṭilum'
will give an idea of Jati mentioned in his text:

जातयोऽष्टादश ज्ञेयास्तासां सप्तस्वराख्यया ।
शुद्धाश्च विकृताश्चैव शेषास्ततसंकरोद्भवाः ॥
षड्जाया मध्यमायाश्च संसर्गात् षड्जमध्यमा ।
षड्जायास्त्वथ गान्धार्या जायते षड्ज कौशिकी ॥
तयोरेव सधंवत्ये षड्जोदीच्यवती भवेत् ।
आसां समध्यमानां तु गान्धारोदीच्य वा भवेत् ॥
गान्धार्या मध्यमायाश्च पञ्चभ्याश्चैव संकरात् ।
सधंवतीनामासां तु मध्यमोदीच्य वा भवेत् ॥
आसां स्याद् रक्तगान्धारी नेषादिचेच्चतुर्थिका ।

आर्षभ्यास्तु भवेदान्ध्री गान्धार्याश्चैव संकरात् ॥
अनयोस्तु सपञ्चम्योर्नादयन्ती प्रजायते ।
सनिषादास्तु गान्धार्यः कुर्युः कर्मारवीमिमाम् ॥
गान्धारी पञ्चमीचैव तथा गान्धार पञ्चमी ।
आर्षभीध्वैवतीवर्जाः कौशिकीमिति संकराः ॥

Brihadesi by 'matanga muni' is a very important
land mark, chronologically this work stands between
'dutilam' and 'sangeet makaranda' by Nārada, that
is, some time between the fourth and the seventh
centuries. Mention of 'grāma rāg' had been chiefly
made by 'Matanga Muni' in his work. But it should
be noted here that the present 'rāgas' are entirely
different from that of the 'grāma-rāg' mentioned by
him in his text. He is also of the opinion that the
Jati generate the grama rāg with the use of predomi-
nating note, *i.e.* 'amsa-svara.' He regards 'rāg' as
one of the seven classes of jatis current in his own
time. *viz:*

१ श्रुतिग्रहस्वरादि समुहाज्जायन्ते जातयः ।
२ यस्माज्जायते रसप्रतीतिरारभ्यते । इति जातयः ।
३ अथवा सकलस्य रागादेर्जन्महेतुत्वाज्जातयः ।
४ यथा नराणां ब्रह्मणत्वादयो जातयः ।

The following verses quoted from his work will
clear the actual idea of jati that was in the mind of
the said author:

ग्रहांशौ तारमन्द्रौ च षाड्वौडुम्बिते तथा ।
अल्पत्वं च बहुत्वं च न्यासोऽपन्यास एव च ॥
ज्ञायते तद्यथा जाति देश जातीय लक्षणा ।
लक्षणं दशकस्यास्य संक्षेपणाभिधीयते ॥

It was matanga, who, for the first time introduced
the word 'rāg' separately in the literature of music,

and that very term 'rāg' now-a-days is supposed to be the life of Indian music. He considered 'rāg' as one of the seven classes of 'jatis' current in his time. He cites 'yastika' the earliest authority, according to whom the jatis were of five kinds and they are as follows:

1. sudha, 2. bhina, 3. vesara, 4. gauda, and 5. sadharita, but in his own time the jatis were of seven kinds, namely:

1. sudha, 2. bhina, 3. gaudika, 4.. rāg-jati, 5. sadharini, 6. bhasajati, and 7. bhbhasajati. The 'rāg-jati' is the fourth in his list. He defines 'rāg-jati' as stated below:

स्वर वर्ण विशेषेण ध्वनिभेदेन वा पुनः ।
रज्यते येन यः कश्चित् स रागः सम्मतः सताम् ॥

He means to say that a combination of notes that are attractive with beautiful and illuminating graces are known as 'rāg-jati.' He also makes a sub-division of the above mentioned jati. In his opinion 'sudha' and 'bhiñaka' have each eight varieties, 'gaudika' has three and 'rāgas' have eight varieties. 'sadharini' is of seven kinds, 'bibhasa' and 'bhasa' are of sixteen and twelve kinds each respectively. He again gives the 'rāg-jati' a different name, such as, 1. 'taki,' 2. 'sawari,' 3. 'malava panchama,' 4. 'khadava,' 5. 'vata-rāg,' 6. 'hindolaka,' and 7. 'takka-kaisika.'

It is evident that the jati gayana was current in India even before the time of Bharat and is gradually developed in association with the different section of the acts of a drama. As a passage of Bharat quoted by Matanga in his work indicates as under:

मुखेतु मध्यामग्रामः षड्जः प्रतिमुखे भवेत्
गर्भे साधारितश्चैवाविमर्शे तु पञ्चमः ।
संहारे कौशिकः प्रोक्तः पूर्व रञ्ज्ेतु षाडवः

Ill. 1. Basanta Rāga. Rajput Miniature, Bikaner, about AD 1800.

चित्रेस्याष्टादशङ्गस्य त्वन्ते कौशिक मध्यमः
शुद्धानां विनियोगज्यं ब्रह्मणा समुदाहृतः ।

That is, in short, the 'madhyma grama' melodies should be used in the 'mukheya,' *i.e.*, in the opening of the drama, the 'sadja-grama' melodies in the 'pratimukhya' stage that is in progression, the 'sadharita' melodies in the stage of its development and the 'panchama-jati' melodies for the 'vimarsa' *i.e.*, conversation.

The names of all the eighteen jatis expounded by all the ancient scholars of music are given below: 1. shadji, 2. ārshavi, 3. gandhari, 4. madhyama, 5. panchama, 6. dhaivati, 7. naishadi, 8. shadja-kaishiki, 9. shadjadi-chyava, 10. shadja-madhyama, 11. raktgāndhari, 12. kaishiki, 13. madhyamodichchava, 14. karmaravi, 15. gāndhara-panchama, 16. andhri, 17. nandayanti, and 18. shadja-panchama.

Nārada Mata

'Sangeet Makaranda' by Nārada is another important text on the theory of Indian music, known as 'nārada mata' comes next to 'brahadesi of matanga.' It is believed that the author Nārada not exactly the same sage Nārada, the mention of whom is very frequently found in puraṇa and upa-puraṇa, lived between the seventh and the eleventh centuries.

Mr. Mangesh Ram Krishana Telang, the editor of the book says, 'Sangeet Makaranda is said to be the work of Nārada on the authority of the manuscript. It is difficult to say any thing with certainty about Nārada's life and time.' It is mentionable here that three works on music are ascribed to Nārada *viz:*

1. 'Nāradi'-siksha,' 2. 'Rāga nirupana,' and 3. 'Sāra saṃhita.' Of these the first is available in print.

Comparing it with the present work, I am of opinion
that the author of both these works are not identical.
The Nāradi siksha appears to be the older work. It
treats more of the 'sāma gana' than later music. As
regards the other two works it is difficult to express
any opinion as the manuscripts of these works are not
available. Another work of this name, sangeet makaranda by Veda, is mentioned in the list of works on
music appearing in the book. But as the name of the
author is Veda and not Nārada, it is likely that it
might be different from the present one.

Nārada for the first time gives a detailed account
and classifies Rāgas into masculine, feminine and
neuter Rāgas. He divides the Rāgas into three
groups *viz:* 1. "मुक्ताङ्ग कम्पिताः" Rāgas which have
quivering "कम्पितगमक" throughout, 2. "अर्धकम्पिताः" Rāgas
which have partial quivering and 3. "कम्पविहीनाः"
Rāgas which are absolutely free from quivering. Here
is a list of the names of the Rāgas that are mentioned
in the text "Sangeet Makaranda":

Masculine Rāgas

Bengal. Soma Rāga. Shree Rāga Bhoopali. Chhaya-
Goud. Sudhdha-Goud. Andoli. Dombuli. Goud.
Karnat. Phadamanji. Sudhdha-Nati. Malabgoul.
Rāgaranga. Chhayanata. Kolahala. Saurastra.
Basanta. Sudhdha-Saranga. Bhairavi. Rāgadwani.

बङ्गालः सोमरागश्च श्रीरागश्च तथैव च ।
भूपाली छायगौडश्च शुद्धहिन्दोलिका तथा ॥५३॥
आन्दोली दोम्बुली चैव गौडः कर्णाटकाह्वयः ।
फडमङ्जी शुद्धनाटी तथा मालवगौलिकः ॥५४॥
रागरङ्गच्छायनाटी रागः कोलाहलस्तथा ।
सौराष्ट्री च वसन्तश्च शुद्धसारंगभैरवी ॥५५॥
रागध्वनिस्तथा ह्येते पुंरागाःपरिकीर्तिताः ।

नारदेन विचित्रेण सन्ति नामानि वक्ष्यते ॥५६॥
(संगीत मकरन्द पृ॰ १८)

Feminine *Rāgas*

Tundi. Turashka-Tundi. Malwari. Mahuri. Pau-
ralika. Kambhari. Bhallati. Saindhavi. Salanga.
Gandhari. Devakri. Desi. Velavali. Bahuli. Gunakri.
Dhurjari. Barathi. Draveri. Hamsi. Gaudi. Narayani.
Ahari. Meghranjani. Misranata.

तुण्डी तुरुष्कतुण्डी च मल्लारी माहुरी तथा ।
पौरालिकी च काम्भारी भल्लाती सॅन्धवी तथा ॥५७॥
सालङ्गाख्या च गान्धारी देवक्री देशिनी तथा ।
वेलावली च बहुली गुण्डक्री घूर्जरी तथा ॥५८॥
वराटी द्रावडी हंसी गौडी नारायणी तथा ।
अहरी मेघरञ्जी च मिश्रनाटा यथा क्रमात् ॥५९॥
(संगीत मकरन्द पृ॰ १८)

Neuter *Rāgas*

Kaisiki. Lalita. Dhannasi. Kurunji. Saurastri.
Draviri-Sudhdha. Nagaverathika. Kaumodaki. Ra-
makri. Saveri. Balahamsa. Samavedi. Sankarave-
ranam.

कौशिकी ललितश्चैव घन्नांशी च कुरञ्जिका ।
सौराष्ट्री द्रावडी शुद्धा तथा नागवराटिका ॥६०॥
कौमोदकी च रामक्री सावेरी च तथैव च ।
बलहंसः सामवेदी शंकराभरणस्तथा ॥६१॥
नपुंसका इति प्रोक्ता रागलक्षणकोविदैः ।
(संगीत मकरन्द पृ॰ १९)

He again classifies the Rāgas into three groups
namely, 'Sampurna, Shadava and Odava,' on the
basis of notes used in them.

Sampurna *Rāgas*

Desakh. Madhmadi. Basanta. Bhairava. Malavi.

Nata-Rāga. Mukhari. Ahari. Balahamsa. Ramakriya.
Baratika.

सम्पूर्णरागो देशाक्षी मध्यमादि: प्रकीर्तित: ।
वसन्तभैरवी शुद्धभैरवी मादित: क्रमात् ॥
सम्पूर्ण मालवीरागो गान्धारादि: प्रकीर्तित: ।
नाटरागश्च सम्पूर्ण: स षड्जादिरुदाहृता: ॥
मुखहारी च सम्पूर्णो धैवतादिनिगद्यते ।
सम्पूर्णश्चाहरी प्रोक्तो मध्यमादिरुपक्रम: ॥
बलहंसश्च सम्पूर्णो गान्धारादि: प्रकीर्तित: ।
वसन्त: शुद्धसंज्ञश्च सषड्जादिरुदाहृता: ॥
रामक्रिया शुद्धसंज्ञा सषड्जादिरुदाहृता: ।
वराटिका शुद्धसंज्ञा सषड्जादिरुपक्रमा: ॥
(संगीत मकरन्द पृ० १६-१७)

Shadava Rāga

Deva-Gandhara. Nilamberi. Shree Rāga. Sudhdha-
Bahuli. Sudhdha Gaul. Lalita. Malavashree. Bhupal.
Padabanji. Gundakri. Kuranji.

षाडवो देवगान्धारो गादिर्वंज्यो निषादक: ।
नीलाम्बरी षाडव: स्याद्गादिर्वंज्यो निषादक: ॥
श्रीराग: षाडवो राग: सषड्जादिर्गर्वजित: ।
शुद्धबहुली मध्मादिर्निवर्ज्यस्तु षाडव: ॥
शुद्धगौल: षाडव: स्यान्निषादादिर्घवर्जित: ।
ललित: षाडवो राग: सादिर्वंज्यो ग च स्वर: ॥
मालवश्री: षाडव: स्यात्षड्जादिश्चरिर्वजित: ।
भूपाल: षाडवो रागो गादि: षड्जविवर्जित: ॥
पडवञ्जी षाडवश्चं रिवज्योंऽपि निषादक: ।
गुण्डक्री षाडवश्चैव गंधारादिर्गवर्जित: ॥
कुरञ्जी षाडवो रागो निवज्यों मध्यमादित: ।
(संगीत मकरंद पृ० १७)

Odava Rāga

Dhannayasi. Saveri. Gurjari. Madhyamadi. Mad-

humadi. Maghranji. Madhyamadhi. Velavali Rama-
kritya Narayani. Paliraura.

धन्यासी श्रौडवः प्रोक्तः सावेरी धविवर्जितः ॥४६॥
श्रौडवो गुर्जरी प्रोक्तः सादिर्वज्यौ रिधौ तथा ।
रिधौ वज्यौ मध्यमादिरौडवा मधुमाधवी ॥४७॥
मेधरंजी मध्यमाधि धनिवज्यौ तथौडवः ।
बेलावल्यौडवः स्यात्तु गादिर्वज्यौ सरोस्वरौ ॥४८॥
रामकृत्यौडवः स्यात्तु गादिर्वज्यौ रिधौस्वरौ ।
नारायणी निषादादिरौडवो धपवर्जितः ॥४६॥
पालिरौडवः षड्जादिर्वज्यौ मध्यम पंचमौ ।

(संगीत मकरंद पृ० १८)

Narada classifies the Ragas mentioned above
according to the theory of time which has also mentioned in his text.

Ragas that are sung in the morning
Gandhar. Devagandhar. Dhanyasi. Saindhavi.
Narayani. Gurjari. Bengal. Patamanjari. Lalita.
Hindola. Shree. Saurastra. Maller. Samavedi. Basant
Sudhdha Bhirava. Velavali. Bhupal. Soma Raga.

गान्धारो देवगान्धारो धन्नासी संधवी तथा ।
नारायणी गुर्जरी च बंगालपटमञ्जरी ॥१०॥
ललितन्दोलश्रीका सौराष्ट्रेयजयसाक्षिकौ ।
माह्लारः सामवेदी च वसन्तः शुद्ध भैरवः ॥११॥
बेलावली च भूपालः सोमरागस्तथैव च ।
एते रागास्तु गातव्याः प्रातःकाले विशेषतः ॥१२॥

(संगीत मकरंद पृ० १५)

Ragas that are sung at mid-day
Shankara-varana. Balahamsa. Desi. Manohari.
Saveri. Dombuli. Kambhoji. Gopikambhoji. Kaisiki.
Madhumadvi. Bahuli. Mukhari. Mangal-Kausika.

शंकराभरणः पूर्वो बलहंसस्तथैव च ।
देशी मनोहरी चैव सावेरी दोम्बुली तथा ॥
काम्भोजी गोपिकाम्भोजी कैशिकी मधुमाधवी ।
बहुलीढ्रयं मुखारी च तथा मंगलकौशिका ॥
एते रागविशेषास्तु मध्याह्ने परिकीर्तिताः ।

(संगीत मकरंद पृ० १५)

Evening Rāgas

Sudhdha-Nata. Salanga. Nati. Sudhdha-Batarika.
Gaulo. Malab-Goud. Shree-Rāga Ahari. Ramakriti.
Ranji. Chaya. Beratika. Dravatika-Desi. Nagavratika.
Karnata. Hayatika.

सुद्धनाटा च सालंगो नाटी शुद्ध वराटिका ।
गौलो मालवगौडश्च श्रीरागइचाहरी तथा ॥
तथा रामकृती रङ्जी छाया सर्ववराटिका ।
वराटिका द्रावटिका देशी नागवराटिका ॥
कर्णाटहयगौडीति इत्येते चंद्रमांशजाः ।

(संगीत मकरंद पृ० १५)

Rāgas that are sung three hours before the sunrise and sunset

देशाक्षी भैरवा शुद्धा नादं यत्प्रहरोद्भवम् ॥
वराटिका तथा शुद्धा द्रावटिराग संज्ञिका ।

(संगीत मकरंद पृ० १५)

Deshakshi. Bhairava Sudhdha. Barathika. Sudhdha
Dravatika.

Rāgas that are sung three hours after the sunset and sunrise
Maliari. Mahuri. Andoli. Ramakriti. Chhayanat.

प्रहरोपरि गातव्या मल्हारी माहुरी तथा ॥
श्रान्दोली रामकृती छायानाटा च रङ्गका ।

(संगीत मकरंद पृ० १५)

Ill. 2. Bhairava Rāga. Rajput Miniature 19th century.

He also describes the advantage and disadvantage of singing Rāgas in proper time.

रागावेलाप्रगानेन रागाणां हिंसको भवेत् ।
यः श्रृणोति स दारिद्री श्रायुनंश्याति सर्वदा ॥२४॥
देवताविषये गीतं पुण्यनामप्रवर्द्धनम् ।
श्राध्यात्मिकेन योगेन सर्वपापप्रणाशनम् ॥२५॥

(संगीत मकरंद पृ० १६)

Kaḷinath Mata. Another important treatise on music is 'Sangeet Ratnākar' by Saranga Deva, who, lived at Daulatabād, formerly known as Deogiri in the North of Nizam's dominions in 1210 to 1247 AD. Though the author had followed the foot-steps of his predecessors denying only the principles of masculine and feminine Rāgas expounded by Nārada Muni in his work 'Sangeet Makaranda,' even then he had included many more new things in his text. He had enumerated two hundred and sixty four Rāgas in all. Out of them twenty Rāgas are main, Upa-rāgas are eight and the rest are subsidiary under the scales which had been accepted by all the previous scholars. Here is the list of the main Rāgas and Upa-rāgas as per the enumeration made by Saranga Deva, in his work 'Sangeet Ratnākar':

पंचधा ग्रामरागाः स्युः पंचगीति समश्रयात् ।
गीतयः पंच शुद्धाद्या भिन्ना गौडी च वेसरा ॥
साधारणोति शुद्धा स्यादवक्रैर्लंलितैः स्वरैः ।
भिन्ना सूक्ष्मैः स्वरैर्वक्रैर्मधुरैर्गमकैर्युता ॥
वेगवद्धिः स्वरैर्वर्णं चतुष्केऽयतिरक्तितः ।
वेगस्वरा रागगीतिवेंसरा चोच्यते बुधैः ॥
चतुर्गीतिगतं लक्षम श्रिता साधारणी मता ।
शुद्धादिगीतियोगेन रागाः शुद्धादयो मताः ॥

(संगीत रत्नाकर पृ० १५०)

Description of Rāgas.   Exact no.

1. Grama Rāga.   30
2. Upa-Rāga.   8
3. Rāga.   20
4. Purva Prasidhdha Rāgangani.   8
5.   ,,   ,,   Bhāsangani.   11
6.   ,,   ,,   Kriyangani.   12
7.   ,,   ,,   Upāngani.   3
8.   ,,   ,,   Bhasa Rāga.   96
9.   ,,   ,,   Bibhasa Rāga.   20
10.   ,,   ,,   Anter Bhasa Rāga.   4
11. Rāgas current in his own time.   13
12. Bhāsangani current in his own time.   9
13. Kriyangāni current in his own time.   3
14. Upangāni current in his own time.   27

                   Total no. of Rāgas.   264

Saranga Deva did not mention the principles or
the basis on which he had accepted the Rāgas, Upa-
Rāgas and also the number he had mentioned in his
work. He has described the Rāgas in detail and
furnished every information regarding the same but
that too without showing any cause. However, a
general information as regards the Rāga with the
rules for its singing are given in his text. This was
commented by Pt. Kali Nath a scholar of a later
period, which is generally known as '*Kali Nath Mata*'
sometimes in the 14th and 15th centuries AD.

The author of *Hanuman Mata* has described the
following six Rāgas and thirty Rāginis as the Bharyas
or wives of the same:

Name of the Rāga   Rāginis attached to it

1. *Bhairava Rāga*   Madhmadi, Bhairavi, Ben-

	gali, Barathi and Saindhavi.
2. *Kausika Rāga*	Todi, Khambhabati, Gouri Gunakari, and Kukubha.
3. *Hindola Rāga*	Velavali, Ramkiri, Deshakhaya, Patamanjari and Lelita.
4. *Deepaka Rāga*	Kedari, Kamoda, Desi, Kanada and Nateka.
5. *Shree Rāga*	Basanti, Malavi, Malasree, Dhannasika and Asaveri.
6. *Megh Rāga*	Mallari, Deshkari, Bhoopali, Gurjari and Tanki.

भरंवः कौशिकइचैव हिन्दोलो दीपकरतथा ।
श्रीरागो मेघरागइच षड़ेते पुरुषाह्वयाः ॥
मध्यमादिभेरबी च बाङ्गाली वराटिका ।
सैन्धवी च पुनर्ज्ञेया भेरवस्य वराङ्गनाः ॥
तोड़ी खम्बावती गौरी गुणक्री ककुभा तथा ।
रागिण्यो रागराजस्य कौशिकइय वराङ्गनाः ॥
वेलावली रामकिरी देशाख्या पटमंजरी ।
ललिता सहिता एता हिन्दोलस्य वराङ्गनाः ॥
केदारी कानड़ा देशी कामोदी नाटिका पुनः ।
दीपकस्य प्रियाः पंच ख्याता रागविशारदैः ॥
वासन्ती मालवी चैब मालश्रीइच धनासीका ।
आशावरी च विज्ञेयाः श्रीरागस्य वराङ्गनाः ॥
मल्लारी देशकारी च भूपाली गुर्जरी तथा ।
टंका च पंचमी भार्य्या मेघरागस्य योषितः ॥

इति हनुमन्मते रागरागिण्यः

The author of *Ragarnava Mata* has quoted the following six Rāgas and thirty Rāginis accordingly:

Name of Rāga	Rāginis attached on it
1. *Bhairava Rāga*	Bengali, Gunakiri, Madhyamadi, Basant and Dhanashree.

2. *Panchama Rāga*   Lalita, Gurjari, Desi, Baradi
                          and Ramkriti.
3. *Nata Rāga*   Nata Narayana, Puwa Gan-
                          dhara Salag, Kedar and
                          Karnatak.
4. *Mallar Rāga*   Megh, Maller, Malkauns,
                          Patamanjari and Asaveri.
5. *Gaud Malab*   Hindola, Tribana, Andhali
                          Gauri, and Patahamsika.
6. *Deshakaya*   Bhoopali, Kudayee, Natik
                          and Velavali.

भैरव: पंचमो नाटो मल्लारो गौड़मालव: ।
देशाख्यश्चेति षड्रागाः प्रोच्यंते लोकविश्रुताः ॥
वाङ्गालीयं गुणकिरी मध्यमादिर्बसन्तकः ।
धनाश्रीश्चेति पंचैते रागाः भैरवसंभ्रयाः ॥
ललिता गुर्जरी देशी वराड़ी रामकृत्तथा ।
मता रागर्णवे रागाः पंचैते पंचमाश्रयाः ॥
नटृनारायणः पूर्व्वं गान्धारः सालगस्तथा ।
ततः केदारकर्णाटौ पंचैते नाटसंभ्रया ॥
मेघमल्लारिका मालकौशिकः पटमंजरी ।
श्राशावरीति बिज्ञेया रागा मल्लारसंभ्रयाः ॥
हिन्दोलस्क्षिवणान्धारी गौरी च पटहंसिका ।
पंचैते रागनामानो गौड़माश्रित्य संस्थिताः ॥
भूपाली च कुड़ायी च कामोदी नाटिका तथा ।
बेलावलीति विज्ञेया रागा देशाख्यसंभ्रया ॥
                                    —इति रागारावि‌मतम्

It can safely be concluded here that the actual
form of music of the Vedic and Paurānic age, was
untraceable even before the time of 'siksha' *i.e.* 300
BC. The Vedic literature contain no explanation
regarding the actual position of the Vedic accents
and poetical metres—the 'Chandas' and their proper
use in Vedic chants,

Regarding the music of the different schools in India, before the beginning of the Christian era till the end of the thirteenth century AD, numerous changes have been made, the then current form of music. Almost all the scholars of the past and present are ignorant of the stages by which the three notes of the Sāma Chant rose to the number seven, nor they can say confidently what relation these seven notes bore to the well known seven notes of the later music. The former were known as 'kristha,' 'prathama,' 'dwitiya,' 'tritiya,' 'chaturtha,' 'mandra,' and 'atiswara.' It is certain that these are in descending order of pitch, but in what exact relation, it is impossible to say.

It is a well known fact that the jatis narrated by Bhārata and his predecessors, and the Rāgas described in Ratnākar are defined in terms of moorchana. So that until there is a consensus of opinion as to the right value of shruti and until it becomes possible to determine the sudha scale of Bhārat, other works and specially of Sangeet Ratnākar, these works are bound to remain sealed books.

The great difficulty which a student of these books meets with at the very outset is that of correctly locating the position of the shrutis and swaras of those ancient treatises. In the absence of a satisfactory solution the remaining portion of these books remain perfectly unintelligible. The grāmas, moorchanas, jatis and lastly the rāgas, have to be evolved, as we know from the sudha and vikrita swaras which again depend upon their respective shrutis.

2

The Origin of Rāga

During the past two hundred years, after Saranga Deva, that is the fourteenth and fifteenth centuries AD, the actual changes that had taken place both in the theory and practice of music are the basis of the modern system of music. The gradual development, additions and modifications, that had been made in different aspects of music were not properly recorded by the experts, either due to constant foreign invasion in the country or lack of proper attention of the music scholars.

India's culture, heritage and intellectual attainment have suffered tremendously since the eleventh century AD. On account of constant foreign invasion. Thousands of books on various subjects containing valuable records at Texila, Nālanda, Varanasi, Sārnath, Mathura, Ujjain and many other seats of ancient culture and learnings were destroyed. Hence the available information is only through the history of that particular period and that too in general without any methodical order of events.

The opinion of some of the leading historians of the ancient Hindu period is, that in India, music had reached its climex during the flourishing reign of the Maurya dynasty and it remained so till the end of the Mahomedan conquest. Some scholars say that the fourteenth and fifteenth centuries are the most important in the development of the Northern schools of music. It was the time of the Mahomedan conquest. Majority of the Emperors did a great deal to extend the practice of music and most of them had musicians attached to their courts. From this time dates the introduction of Persian models into the music of India.

The Mahomedans, as a ruling nation, came in contact with the people of India for the first time in the eleventh century and since then the system of music of the country had been undergoing a change. The Mahomedans did not encourage the theory of the art, but they patronized practical musicians and were themselves instrumental in composing and introducing several styles of songs and devised new forms of musical instruments. It is also related by Mahomedan historians of that age, that, when Dacca was invaded by Allauddin Khilji in 1294 AD, and the conquest of South India was accomplished in 1310 AD by his general, Malik Kafur, music was in such a flourishing condition that the musicians and their Hindu preceptors were patronised and employed in service and they settled in the North.

It is to be mentioned here that Hazrat Amir Khusru—the celebrated Persian poet and musician, came to India during the reign of Allauddin Khilji and the active part he took in developing the Indian melodies is noteworthy. By a judicious combination of Persian 'makamats' and Indian 'rāga,' he had introduced many derivative melodies hitherto known

to the musicians of India in his time. It is also said
that Amir is also responsible for the introduction to
Indian music the 'rāgas' namely, Yaman, Firdos,
Fargana, Sarparda, Zilaph and many others.

Nāyak Gopāl was a contemporary of Amir Khusru.
He was acknowledged by all, to be the master in his
art. He had a large number of disciples. The fame
of his perfection and consummate skill in music
moved the Sultan Allauddin, who invited him to
his court to give performance there, which the nāyak
did with great pleasure and also with minute
accuracy.

It is apparent that in Northern India the Mahomedans proved to be a great patrons of fine arts and
specially of music in its real sense and value. They
brought with them the music of their own country
which was assimilated with the music of India. Thus
new melodies, new styles of interpretations, new types
of songs and also new 'tālas' were introduced.

Let us now consider the common and popular
works on music that were in vogue then. One of
such is known as 'sangeet darpana.' This work was
compiled by Pt. Dāmodar Misra, who, was a successor
to 'sāranga dèva' and predecessor of Pt. Lochana
of the fifteenth century. The author of 'sangeet
darpana' had only followed the basic principles laid
down by 'sāranga deva' and introduced the system
of classification of 'rāga and rāgini' in his own way.
This system of music was current in India for more
than a century and a half and is known as 'Shiva mata.'

Music has always been affected by the changes
that have taken place in the country from time to
time. Yet the fundamental principles are still almost
the same as they were about a century before. The

Ill. 3. Hindola Rāga. Rajput Miniature 19th century.

attention of the scholars of the day is drawn to the fact that the problem of the ancient 'rāga and rāgini' system and classification of the 'rāginis' needs a detailed study and research.

It is possible that the author of 'Shiva Mata' might have tried to introduce his own views in the name of 'Shiva' the master of the three fold arts of music, whom almost every Hindu worships. He might have done all this with the object of having a wide spread of the system of Rāgas and Rāginis introduced by him. It is also probable that he might be an ascetic or Yogi so, whatever he has realised through his meditation, he might have included in his text for the benefit of the lovers of music in the name of 'Shiva' so that the people may not have the least objection to it.

The following six Rāgas and thirty six Rāginis are mentioned in his text 'Sangeet Darpana' (page 72-73).

श्रीरागोऽथ वसन्तश्च भैरवः पञ्चमस्तथा
मेघरागो बृहन्नाटः षडेते पुरुषाह्वयाः ॥

1. Shree Rāga, 2. Basanta, 3. Bhairava, 4. Panchama, 5. Megha-Rāga and 6. Brihannata.

मालश्री त्रिवणी गौरी केदारी मधुमाधवी ।
ततः पाहाड़िका ज्ञेया श्रीरागस्य वराङ्गनाः ॥
देशी देवगिरी चैव वराटी तोडिका तथा ।
ललिता चाऽथ हिन्दोली वसन्तस्य वराङ्गनाः ॥
भैरवी गुर्ज्जरी रामकिरी गुणकिरी तथा ।
बाङ्गाली सैन्धवी चैव भैरवस्य वराङ्गनाः ॥
विभाषा चाऽथ भूपाली कर्णाटी वडहंसिका ।
मालवी पटमञ्जर्य्याः सहैताः पञ्चमाङ्गनाः ॥
मल्लारी सौरटी चैव सावेरी कौशिकी तथा ।
गान्धारी हरश्रृङ्गारा मेघरागस्य योषितः ॥

कामोदी चेंव कल्याणी आभिरी नाटिका तथा ।
सारङ्गी नट्टहम्बीरा नट्ट नारायाणङ्गनाः ॥

1. Malashree, 2. Tribani, 3. Gouri, 4. Kedari, 5.
Madhumadhavi, 6. Pahadika, 7. Desi, 8. Devagiri,
9. Barathi, 10. Todi, 11. Lalita, 12. Hindoli, 13.
Bhairavi, 14. Gurjari, 15, Ramkiri, 16. Gunakiri,
17. Bengali, 18. Saindhabi, 19. Bibhasa, 20. Bhupali,
21. Karnati, 22. Badahamsika, 23. Malavi, 24. Pata-
manjari, 25. Mallari, 26. Sorathi, 27. Saveri, 28.
Kausiki, 29. Gandhari, 30. Harasringara, 31. Kamodi,
32. Kalyani, 33. Abhiri, 34. Sarangi, 35. Natta-
Hambira, 36. Natta-Narayana.

He has also classified the Rāgas and Rāginis which
he wishes to be sung in different hours of the day and
night. The following Rāgas and Rāginis are to be
sung early at dawn, morning, at noon, forenoon and
in the evening.

Rāgas that are to be sung in the morning
Madhumadhavi. Deshakhya. Bhupali. Bhairavi.
Velavali. Mallari. Ballari. Soma. Gurjari. Dhanashree. Malavashree. Megha-Rāga. Punchama. Desh-
kari. Bhairava. Lalita. Basanta.

मधुमाधवी च देशाख्या भूपाली भैरवी तथा ।
वेलावली च मल्लारी वल्लारी सोमगुर्ज्जरी ॥
धनाश्रीर्मलवश्रीश्च मेघरागश्च पञ्चमः ।
देशकारी भैरवश्च ललिता च वसन्तकः ॥
एते रागाः प्रगीयन्ते प्रातरारभ्य नित्यशः ॥

Rāgas to be sung three hours after the sunrise
Gurjari. Kausika. Saveri. Patamanjari. Reva.
Gunakiri. Bhairavi. Ramakiri. Saurathi.

गुज्जरी कौशिकश्चैव सावेरी पटमञ्जरी ।
रेवा गुणकिरी चैव भैरवी रामकिर्यपि ॥
सोराटी च तथा गेया प्रथम प्रहरोत्तरम् ॥

Rāgas to be sung at noon

Bairathi. Todika. Kamodi. Kudayi. Gandhari. Nagasabdi. Desi. Shankarabharana.

वैराटी तोड़िका चैव कामोदी च कुड़ायिका ।
गान्धारी नागशब्दी च तथा देशी विशेषतः ।
शंकराभरणो गेयो द्वितीय प्रहरात् परम् ॥

Rāgas that are to be sung in afternoon

Shree Rāga. Malab. Gouri. Triban. Nata-Kalyan. Saranga. Nata. Kedari. Karnat Abheri. Badahamsa. Pahadi.

श्रीरागो मालवाह्वयश्च गौरी त्रिवणसंज्ञिका ।
नट्टकल्याणसंज्ञश्च सारङ्गनट्टको तथा ॥
सर्वे नाटाश्च केदारी कर्णटयाभीरिका तथा ।
वड़हंसी पहाड़ी च तृतीयप्रहरात् परम् ॥

The author again gives a detailed description of the following Rāgas and their pictorial illustrations which are added in this text:

राग भैरवः—

धैवतांशप्रहन्यासोरिपहीनत्त्वसागतः ।
भैरवः सतु विज्ञेयो धैवतादिकमूर्च्छनः ।
विकृतो धैवतो यत्र औड़वः परिकीर्तितः ॥

भैरव राग ध्यानः—

गङ्गाधरः शशिकला तिलक त्रिनेत्रः
सर्पैर्विभूषिततनूर्गज कृत्तिवासाः ।
भास्वत्त्रिशूलकर एष नृमुण्डधारी
शुभ्राम्बरो जयति भैरव आदि रागः ॥

श्रीरागः—

श्रीरागः स च विख्यातः सत्रयेण विभूषितः ।
पूर्णः सर्व्वगुणोपेतो मूर्च्छना प्रथमा मता ॥
कचित्तु कथयन्त्येनमृषभत्रयसंयुतम् ॥

श्रीरागध्यानः—

अष्टादशाब्दः स्मरचारुमूर्त्तिः
धीरो लसत्पल्लवकर्णपूरः ।
षड्जादि सेव्योऽरुणवस्त्रधारी
श्रीराग एष क्षितिपालमूर्त्तिः ॥

मेघ रागः—

मेघः पूर्णो धत्रयः स्यादुत्तरायतमूर्च्छनः ।
विकृतो धंवतो ज्ञेयः भृङ्गाररसपूरकः ॥

मेघ राग ध्यानः—

नीलोत्पलाभवपुरिन्दु समान वक्तः ।
पीताम्बरस्तृषित चातकवाच्य मानः ।
पीयूषमन्दहसितो घन मध्यवर्त्ती ।
वीरेषु राजति युवा किल मेघ रागः ॥

राग पंचचमः—

रागः पञ्चमको ज्ञेयः पहीनः षाडवो मतः ।
प्रथमा मूर्च्छना यत्र षड्जत्रयविभूषितः ।
केचिद्वहन्ति सम्पूर्णः भृङ्गाररसपूरकः ॥

राग पंचचम ध्यानः—

रक्ताम्बरो रक्त विशालनेत्रः
भृङ्गारयुक्तस्तरुणो मनस्वी ।
प्रभात काले विजयी च नित्यं
सदा प्रियः कोकिलमञ्जु भाषी ॥

The system laid down by Nārada, Hanumān and
Shiva, fundamentally differs from the propositions

narrated by Bharat and Saranga Deva or Kaḷi Nath. Mention of Hanumān and Ragarnava mata is found in the text of 'Shiva mata,' but both these authors disagree with the system of classification of the Rāgas and Rāginis that has already been explained.

These points lead one to believe that Nārad, Hanumān, Shiva and particularly the author of 'Rāgarnava mata' might have borrowed all materials for their respective books from some older works, which are now not traceable, or all of them might have intended to introduce their own ideas regarding the system of classification of 'rāga and rāgini' which ofcourse, they did with creditably.

None of the scholars of the medieval age, neither defined the term 'rāga and rāgini' nor stated any where in their respective texts, the reasons, if any for such fanciful classification which were full of controversy. Hence, the authors of a later period excluded this system from their music literature and included in their respective works the system of 'jānak-jānya' or 'mela or rāga,' which is current even to-day.

Damoder Misra was of the opinion that Bhairava Rāga is Odava—Odava, Rishava and Panchama are omitted in ascent and descent, but in the opinion of later scholars and also according to the current practice it is a Sampurna—Sampurna Rāga. This goes to prove that the medieval Rāgas and the system of their classification were going out of date and so, the scholars of later period did not follow them and consequently these old systems which were full of disparity, were uncared by the scholars of later age and also by the educated students, who were also in search of a better method based on scientific lines.

In spite of all these disputes—the works of Nārada

and Damoder Misra should be studied by all advanced
students of music. These works deserve a detailed
study and research. They have referred many other
scholars of the by-gone-age whose names are not
generally found in any other texts on music.

Damodar Misra has quoted in his text the verses
from Hanumān, Ragarnava and Someshwar mata as
the supporters of his theory. These quotations prove
that in spite of the difference of opinion and disagreement on the principle of classification of Rāgas and
Rāginis still all of them unanimously agreed to that
very system that was current then. Almost all of them
accepted six main Rāgas and thirty six Rāginis except
the author of Ragarnava mata, who, only accepts
thirty Rāginis and six Rāgas different from others.

The author of Someshwar mata is of the opinion
that each Rāga and its Rāginis should be sung in the
specific season of the year for example:

श्रीरागो रागिणीयुक्तः शिशिरे गीयते बुधैः ।
वसन्तः ससहायस्तु वसन्ततौ प्रगीयते ॥
भैरवः ससहायस्तु ऋतौ ग्रीष्मे प्रगीयते ।
पंचमस्तु तथा गेयो रागिण्या सह शारदे ॥
मेधरागो रागिणीभिर्युक्तो वर्षासु गीयते ।
नट्टनारायणो रागो रागिण्या सह हेमका ॥

That is he means to say that the Rāgas and Rāginis
are to be sung in the following way:

1. Shree Rāga and its Rāginis are to be sung in the
months of January and February that is in the end
of winter season (शिशिर).

2. Basanta Rāga and its Rāginis should be sung in
the months of March and April, that is in the spring
season (वसन्त).

3. Bhairava Rāga and its Rāginis are sung in the

months of May and June, that is in the summer season (ग्रीष्म).

4. Megha Rāga and its Rāginis must be sung in the months of July and August, that is in Rains (वर्षा).

5. Panchama Rāga and its Rāginis are to be sung in the months of September and October, that is in autumn (शरद).

6. Natta Narayana Rāga and its Rāginis must be sung in the months of November and December that is in the winter season (हेमन्त).

It is also found in Ayeen-e-Akbery or Akber's Regulations for the Government of Hindustan by Abul Fazl Allami, translated by Franci Gladevin (vide p. 727).

"Singing was invented by Mahadeva and Parvati. That the first had five mouths from each of which issued a musical mode in the following order:

1. Shree Rāga. 2. Basant Rāga. 3. Behrown Rāga. 4. Panchama Rāga. 5. Megh Rāga. To these they add Natta Narayana which they attribute to Parvati. These six modes they call Rāga and each has several varieties, the following six are most common.

1. Varieties of Shree Rāga
1. Malavi, 2. Triveni, 3. Gauri, 4. Kedari, 5. Madhmadi, 6. Vihari or Behari.

2. Varieties of Basanta
1. Desi, 2. Devagiri, 3. Vairati, 4. Todi, 5. Lalita, 6. Hindola.

3. Varieties of Behrown
1. Madhyamadi, 2. Bhairavi, 3. Bengali, 4. Varatika, 5. Saindhavi, 6, Punarjneya or Poonargeya.

4. *Varieties of Panchama*
1. Maller, 2. Saurastri, 3. Asaveri, 4. Kausika, 5. Gandhari, 6. Harasringara.

5. *Varieties of Megha Rāga*
1. Mallar, 2. Saurashtri, 3. Asaveri, 4. Kausiki 5. Gandhari, 6. Harashingara.

6. *Varieties of Natta-Narayāna*
1. Kamodi, 2. Kalyan, 3. Ahiri, 4. Sudhdha-Nata, 5. Salaka (Saluk), 4. Nata Hambir.

He says that some make only four varieties of each Rāga, others in the place of Basant, Panchama and Megh use Malakausika, Hindola and Deepaka, and make five varieties of each and the rest instead of Basant, Behrown, Panchama and Megh use Sudhdha Behrown, Hindola, Deshkar and Sudhdha-Nata.

Abul Fazl generally follows the authorities according to whom six Rāginis are assigned to each Rāga. But the Rāginis that belong to Bhairava are given with exact order of the list of Hanumān according to whom each Rāga has only five Rāginis.

A common opinion among the majority of the musicians, Hindu and Muslim both alike, is that the 'rāgas and rāginis' are created by God and Goddess. It is very difficult to say any thing definitely how far they are correct in their statement, perhaps which is more or less based upon the conjectures of the authors of Purāns and Up-Purāns. The following is an interesting story quoted from 'adbhuta-rāmāyana about the sage Nārada which is nothing but a constructive criticism to a devotee of this art with a real appreciation.

'Once Nārada the great hermit felt proud that he

Ill. 4. Megha Rāga. Rajput Miniature, Mewar, about AD 1650.

had mastered the divine art of music, Lord Vishnu, the omniscient—the protector of all living beings, in order to curb his pride, took Nārado along with him to visit the abode of the Gods in heaven. They soon entered a specious building in which, were numerous handsome men and young beautiful women—but all of them were weeping over their deformed limbs. Vishnu stopped there and enquired of them the cause of their misery. The reply was that they were none but the 'rāgas and rāginis' created by Maheshwara but while a wise man named Nārada, ignorant of the science and the art of music and also unskilled in performance had sung recklessly and as a result of that their features were distorted and their limbs raptured. They also said that unless Tumburu—the master of this art sings them properly, there was no hope of their being restored to their proper form. Nārad was very much ashamed for his vanity, so he knelt down with folded hands before Vishnu to apologise.'

It is more interesting to know that the author of *Sangeet Ratnavali* of a later period, supported the system laid down by Saranga Deva without the least disagreement in this connection.

It is possible therefore that the author of the book might have either followed him blindly or borrowed every material from his work. So this book does not stand in need of any minute observation.

Pandit Lochana—The author of *Raga Tarangini* lived in the district of Mithila. The exact date is more or less doubtful—still there is ample evidence for it. As the author himself quotes from another poet named 'Vidyapati,' who, lived about the end of the fourteenth century. Moreover Lochana mentions in his work the Rāgas like 'Yaman' and 'Fardost' that were introduced by the Mahomedans. Therefore it is certain that *Raga Tarangini* must have been compiled some time in the fifteenth century or by the end of the 14th century and before 1660 AD.

Lochana for the first time left behind the old traditions of 'Grama,' 'Murchana' and 'Jati gayana' and gave place to the 'Janya-Janak' or 'Thata the Mela' theory. He regards the following 'Thatas' to be the parent scales and then classifies his 'Janya Rāgas'— numbered seventy five only under them, and totally omitted the poetic theory of Rāga and Rāgini. Pictorial illustrations of such Rāgas and 'Rāginis' as imagined by the then artists can be gathered from medieval literature, paintings and sketches.

The following are the twelve Thatas expounded by Lochana:

1. Bhairava, 2. Todi, 3. Gauri, 4. Karnat, 5. Kedar, 6. Yaman, 7. Saranga, 8. Megha, 9. Dhannasree, 10. Purva, 11. Mukhari and 12. Deepaka.

He next classifies his seventy five 'Janya Rāgas' under the 'Thata system' quoted below:

Name of the Thata.   Rāgas derived from it.

1. *Bhairavi*   Bhairavi and Nilamberi.

नीलांबरी सदा गेया भैरवी रागिणी स्थितौ ।

2. *Todi*   Todi.

टोडी मुरागिणी कापि स्वस्थितौ सैव गीयते ।

3. *Gouri*   Malab,   Shree-Rāga,   Chati
                       Gouri,   Pahadi-Goudi,   Desi
                       Todi, Desikari Goura, Triban,
                       Multani, Dhanashree, Basant,

Bhairava, Bibhas, Ramkali
Gurjali, Bahuli, Reva, Bhatihar,
Khat, Malab-Panchama, Jaith-
sree, Asaveri, Devagandhar,
Sindhi-Asaveri, Gunakari.

मालवः स्यान्गुणमयः श्रीगौरी च विशेषतः ।
चैती गौरी तथा प्रोक्ता पहाडीगौरिका पुनः ॥
देशीटोडी देशकारो गौरो रागेषु सत्तमः ।
त्रिवणः स्यान्मूलतानी धनाश्रीश्च वसंतकः ॥
गौरा भैरवरागश्च विभासो रागसत्तमः ।
रामकली तथागेया गुर्जरी बहुली ततः ॥
रेवा च भटियारश्च षड्रागश्च तथोत्तमः ।
मालवः पंचमः किञ्चजयंतश्रीश्च रागिणी ॥
असावरी तथा ज्ञेया देवगांधार एव च ।
सिंधी आसावरी ज्ञेया ज्ञेया गुणकरी तथा ॥
गौरी संस्थानमध्ये तु एते रागा व्यवस्थिताः ।

4. *Karnat*

Karnat, Bageshwari, Kamach,
Sorath, Paraj, Maru, Jaijaibanti,
Kukubha, Kamode, Kedar,
Malab-Kausik, Hindol, Sughrai,
Adana, Gara-Kanada, Shree
Rāga.

षाडवः कानरो रागो देशी विख्यातिमागतः ।
वागीश्वरी कानरश्च खमाइची तु रागिणी ॥
सोरठः परजो मारु जैजयंती तथा परा ।
ककुभोऽपि च कामोदः कामोदी लोकमोदिनी ॥
केदारी रागिणी रम्या गौरः स्यात् मालकौशिकः ।
हिन्दोलः सुघराई स्यादडानो राग सत्तमः ॥
गारेकानरनामा च श्रीरागश्च सुखावहः ।
कर्णाटसंस्थिताबेते रागाः सन्तीति निश्चितम् ॥

5. *Kedar*

Kedar-Nata, Abhir-Nata, Kham-

bhavati,   Sankarabheranam,
Behagra,   Hamir,   Shyam,
Chayanat, Bhupali, Bhimpalasi,
Kausik, Maru.

केदारस्वरसंस्थाने   श्रुतः   केदारनाटकः   ।
आभीरनाटनामा   च   गेयो   रागस्तथापरः   ॥
रवंबावती   ततो   ज्ञेया   शंकराभरणस्तथा   ।
चिह्नगराच   हम्बीरः   श्यामः   श्रुतिमनोहरः   ॥
छायानटश्च   भूपाली   ज्ञेया   भांपलासिका   ।
कौशिकश्च   तथा   गेयो   मारु   रागो   विचक्षणैः   ॥

6. *Yaman*   Yaman, Sudhdha-Kalyan-Puria,
                          Jait-Kalyan.

ईमन   स्वरसंस्थाने   शुद्धकल्याण   ईरितः   ।
पूरिया   विदिता   लोके   जयत्कल्याण   एव   च   ॥

7. *Saranga*   Saranga, Pata-manjari, Brinda-
                          bani-Saranga, Samanta-Saran-
                          ga, Badahamsa.

सारंग   स्वरसंस्थाने   प्रथमा   पटमंजरी   ।
वृन्दावनी   तथा   ज्ञेया   सामंतो   वडहंसकः   ॥

8. *Megha*   Megh-Maller,   Gaud-Saranga,
                          Bilaval, Alahiya Sudhdhasuhali,
                          Desh, Chayanat.

मेघरागस्य   संस्थाने   मेघो   मल्लार   एव   च
गौरसारंगनाटौ   च   रागो   बेलावली   तथा
अलहिया   तथा   ज्ञेया   शुद्धसूहव   एव   च
देशीसूहव   देशाखौ   शुद्धनाटस्तथैव   च

9. *Dhanashree*   Dhanasree, Lalit.

धनाश्री   स्वरसंस्थाने   धनाश्रीर्ललितस्तथा   ।

10. *Purva*   Purva.

पूर्वायाः स्वरसंस्थाने पूर्बेंवपरिगीयते

11. *Mukhari*   Mukhari.

मुखारी स्वरसंस्थाने मुखारीपरिगीयते ।

12. *Deepaka*   Deepaka.

The Rāgas mentioned ere now by Lochana, are also enlisted in the works by the modern scholars, and majority of them are practically sung by the musicians of these days.

Thus his work is one of the greatest historical importance to the students of music. It should be noted here that most of the 'Janya Rāgas' narrated by him seem to have retained their original form even to-day. This work is on prosody and the author did not give any detailed account of the 'Janya-Janak,' 'Mala' or 'Rāga.' He also did not care to explain fully the principles or the basis on which he had accepted the 'Thata' or 'Mela' system. This was followed by the work of *'Hridaya Narayana Deva'*—of Garha-Desa about the year 1660 AD. His work namely 'Hridaya Kautuka' and 'Haridaya Prakash' are important, so far as the subject matter of Swara Prakarana, definition, of Rāga and the system of classification of Rāgas are concerned.

The author himself had introduced a new Rāga and has used two new or different Swaras—notes for the Rāga newly composed by him with two different new notes so called newly added.

He had accepted the twelve 'Thata' of 'Rāg Tarangini' and added his own composition to it. But the system of arrangement of Thata is absolutely different from his predecessor. Here is the list of the

Rāgas which the author had put into different groups according to the notes, namely, Suddha and Vikrita used in them.

Group no. 1.   Sudhdha Mela.   Bhairavi Mela.

सांशन्यासा च सम्पूर्णा षड्जादि भैरंवी भवेत्
—हृदय प्रकाश ।

शुद्धाः सप्त स्वरा रम्या वादनीयाः प्रयत्नतः ।
तेन वादन मात्रेण भैरवी जायते शुभा ॥
अन्ये तु भैरवी रागे धैवतं कोमलं विदुः ।
तदशुद्धं यतस्तादृङ् नायं रागोऽनुरंजकः ॥
—हृदय कौतुक ।

Group no. 2.   Tivratara Gandhara.   Karnat.

कर्णाटिस्तत्र संपूर्णः षड्जादिः परिकीर्तितः ।
—हृदय प्रकाश ।

शुद्धाः सप्तस्वरास्तेषु गान्धारो मध्यमस्य चेत् ।
गृह्लाति द्वे श्रुती गीता कर्णाटी जायते तदा ॥
—हृदय कौतुक ।

Group no. 3.   Komala Dhaivata.   Mukhari.

घकोमला मुखारी स्यात्पूर्णा धादिकमूर्छना ।
—हृदय प्रकाश ।

शुद्धाः सप्त स्वरास्तेषु धैवतः कोमलो भवेत् ।
वीणायां जायते शुद्धा मुखारीसंस्थितिस्तदा ॥
—हृदय कौतुक ।

Group no. 4.   Komala Dhaivata and Rishava Tivra
Gandhara, and nishad.   Todi.

कोमलर्षभधैवतौ, तीव्रतरगान्धार निषादौच ।
कोमलर्षभधा पूर्णा गांशा तोडी निरूप्यते ॥
—हृदय प्रकाश ।

शुद्धाः सप्तस्वराः कार्यारिधौ तेषु च कोमलौ ।
तोडी सुरागिणी ज्ञेया ततो गायकनायकैः ॥
—हृदय कौतुक ।

Group no. 5.   Gandhara and Nishada.   Kedar

भूपालीचेति, केदारः संपूर्णो गादि मूर्छनाः ।
एवं सति निषादश्चेत् काकली भवति स्फुटम् ।
वीणायां व्यक्तिमाधत्ते केदारी रागिणीतदा ॥

Group no. 6.   Tivratara Gandhara, Dhaivata and
               Nishada.   Yaman.

तत्रेमनः पूरियाख्यौ जयत्कल्याण एव च ।
चतुर्थः शुद्ध कल्याणः पूर्णस्तत्रे मनो यथा ।
एवं सति च संस्थाने मध्यमः पंचमस्य चेत् ।
गृह्णाति दे श्रुतो राग ईमनो जायते तदा ॥

Group no. 7.   Tivratara Gandhara Dhaivata and
               Nishada.   Megh.

धनिषादौ च शार्ङ्गस्य कर्णाटस्य गमौ यदि ।
भवेतां रागराजन्यो मेघरागः प्रजायते ॥

Group no. 8.   Tivratama, Gandhara, Madhyama
               and Nishada.   Hridaya Rama.

गस्यतीव्रतमत्वेऽथ तथा तीव्रतमौ मनी ।
इहैवोत्प्रैक्षितापूर्णा हृदयाद्वारिमोच्यते ॥

Group no. 9.   Rishava Dhaivata Komala with Tiv-
               ratara Gandhara and Nishada.
                                       Gouri.

Group no. 10. Ati Trivatama Gandhara Tivratara
               Dhaivata-Madhyama and Kakali
               Nishada.   Saranga.

एवं सति च गान्धारः शुद्धमध्यमतां ब्रजेत् ।
धश्च शुद्धनिषादः स्यात् सारंगो जायते तदा ॥
अतितीव्र तमौगाख्यो मधौ तीव्र तरौ कृ ।
यत्रनिः काकलि तत्रा सारंगः पटमंजरी ॥

Group no. 11.   Tivratara   Gandhara,   Madhyama
            Dhaivata and Kakali Nishada.

                                              Purva.

ईमनस्वर संस्थाने निषादप्रथमांश्रुतिम ।
गृह्णाति धैवतश्चेषा पूर्वायाः स्वरसंस्थितिः ।

Group no. 12.   Tivratara Gandhara Madhyama Ri-
            shava and Kakali Nishada.

                                          Dhanashree.

गमौ तीव्रतरौ यत्र रिधौ कोमल संज्ञकौ ।
निषादः काकली, पूर्णाधनाश्रीस्तत्र कीर्तिता ॥
रिषभः कोमलो गस्तु द्वे श्रुती मध्यमस्य चेत् ।
गृह्णाति द्वे श्रुती मश्च पंचमस्य विशेषतः ॥
धैवतः कोमलो निश्च पड्जस्य द्वे श्रुती तदा ।
गृह्णाति रागिणी रम्या धनाश्रीर्जायते तदा ॥

The following Rāgas have been described by Hridaya Narayana Deva in his text.

1. Saindhavi, 2. Kukubha, 3. Bhairavi, 4. Nilamberi, 5. Karnat, 6 Jijabanti, 7. Saurastra, 8. Sugh-
arai, 9. Kamode, 10. Adana, 11. Bageshwari, 12.
Mukhari, 13. Todi, 14. Kedar, 15. Shyam-Nata, 16.
Khambavati, 17. Hamir, 18. Shankaravaranam, 19.
Jayat-Kedar, 20. Puriya Kedar, 21. Behagara, 22.
Ahir-Nata, 23. Maru, 24. Bhimpalasi, 25. Chayanata,
26. Kedar-Nata, 27. Malkausika, 28. Bhoopali, 29.
Yaman, 30. Puriya Kalyan, 31. Jait-Kalyan, 32. Sudh-
dha Kalyan, 33. Megh, 34. Sudhdha-Nata, 35. Nata,
36. Devagiri, 37. Gaod-Saranga, 38. Alahiya, 39.
Deva-Bharan, 40. Desakh, 41. Gaud-Maller, 42.
Suhab, 43. Madhyamadi, 44. Maller, 45. Hridaya
Rama, 46. Gauri, 47. Multan-Dhanashree, 48. Shree-
Rāga, 49. Shad Rāga, 50. Chaiti-Goure, 51. Basant,
52. Jayashree, 53. Ramkali, 54. Paraj, 55. Panchama,

Ill. 5. Madhumādhavī Rāginī. Rajput Miniature, Amber, 18th century.

56. Gandhar, 57. Asaveri, 58. Desi-Todi, 59. Bhairava, 60. Bahuli, 61. Gurjari, 62. Gaud, 63. Gunakari, 64. Desh-Kala, 65. Malashree, 66. Bibhas, 67. Tribani, 68. Sarang, 69. Pata-Manjari, 70. Samant, 71. Bada Hamsa, 72. Purva, 73. Dhanashree.

संधव, भैरवी, नीलांबरी, कर्णाट कुकुभा, जिजावंती, सौराष्ट्री सुघराई, कामोद, अडाना, वागेश्वरी, मुखारी, टोडी, केदार, श्यामनट, खंवावती, हमीर, शंकराभरण, जयतकेदार, पूरिया, केदार, विहागरा, अहीरनट, मारु, भीम-पलाशी, छायानट, केदारनट, मालकौश, भूपाली, ईमन, पूरिया कल्याण, जयतकल्याण, शुद्ध कल्याण, मेघ, शुद्ध नट, नट, देवगिरी, गौर सारंग, अलहिया, देवाभरण.

देशरव, गौडमल्लार, सूहव, मध्यमादी, मल्लार, हृदयरमा, गौरी, मुलतानी, धनासरी, श्रीराग, षड्राग, चेतीगौरी, वसंत, जयश्री, रामकली, परज, पंचम, गान्धार, असावरी, देशीतोडी, भैरव, वहुली, गुर्जरी, गौड, गुणकरी, देशकाल, मालश्री, बिभास, त्रिवण, सारंग, पटमंजरी, सामंत, बडदंस, पूर्वा, धनाश्री.

Regarding the 'Rāga Deepaka'—which was related by Lochana had been precluded by Hridaya Narayana Deva. It is therefore possible that in his time 'Rāga Deepaka' was not current; that is, why he might have dropped it from his text.

The most important treatise of the 17th century is Sangeet Parijat by Pundit Ahobala. It is believed that he was a South Indian Pundit but he had come in contact with the Northerners and had settled there. His work shows that he has dealt more with the music of North India and less with the South Indian music.

The system expounded by him in his text is on the North Indian music but several Rāgas that are popular even to-day in South Indian music have been mentioned there. Sir W. Ousley in his Oriental Collections, Vol., I., says that Sangeet Parijat was translated into Persian by Pundit Deva Nath, son of

Basudeo in the year 1724 AD. I have seen a copy of
the Persian translation in the Rampur State library.
The copy bears the seal of the curator of Emperor
Mohammad Shah's library. We know that Mohammad Shah ascended the throne of Delhi in the year
1719 AD. Parijat is freely quoted by Pundit Bhava
Bhatta, in his well known work Sangeet Anupa Vilas.
Bhava Bhatta's father, was in the service of the Emperor Shahjahan, and he himself was attached to the
court of Raja Anupa Singh of Bikaner, who was a
contemporary of Aurangzeb. There is reason therefore to believe that Ahobala had some acquaintance
with the famous Southern treatises.

Rāga Vibodha was written by Soma Nath, in 1610
AD. These facts would go to prove that Sangeet Parijat was compiled some time in the latter half of the
17th century. References made here and there by
Soma Nath for certain Rāgas, in connection with the
system of 'Mela' is enough to prove that in his time,
the method of classification of Rāgas under 'Thata'
was prevalent. He himself has described about one
hundred and twenty Rāgas in his text and has mentioned in detail the notes that are used in them, as for
example, the Aroha (ascent) and Avaroha (descent),
the Graha and Nyasa and also the Murchanas.

The verses that are noted below will form an idea
about the same.

धनाश्रीर्मालवश्रीश्च रक्तहंसो वसन्तकः ।
देशाख्यो देशकारी च भूपाली प्रसभस्तथा ॥३४१॥
मध्यमादिः कोल्लहासो बङ्गाली भैंरवस्तथा ।
नारायणो विभासश्च प्रतार्गेया इमे बुधैः ॥३४२॥
गुर्जरी रेवगुप्तिश्च कौमारी कज्जली तथा ।
शंकराभरणस्तोडी सोरठी रामकृत्तथा ॥३४३॥

नादरामक्रियारागो वेलावली कुडाविका ।
गुणकारी जयश्रीश्च तथैव शिववल्लभा ॥३४४॥
एते रागाः प्रगीयन्ते प्रथमप्रहरोत्तरम् ॥३४५॥
हंसाख्यो दीपको रागाः काम्भोदी कंकणस्तथा ।
सारङ्गो देव गान्धारी रागो देवगिरिः परा ॥३४६॥
ऐरावतोऽर्जुनो रागो रत्नावली ततः परम् ।
असावरी च हिंदोलो मनोहरस्तथैव च ॥३४७॥
वैजयन्ती तथा रागाः सर्वश्चैव वराटिकाः ।
एते रागाः प्रगीयन्ते द्वितीयप्रहरोत्तरम् ॥३४८॥
घण्टरागस्तथा ढक्कः श्रीरागः कोकिलः पुनः ।
सौदामिनी कुरङ्गश्च त्रिवेणी च सुरालयः ॥३४९॥
पूर्वी विहङ्गडो रागः सामन्त कुमुदस्तथा ।
वडहंसः पहाड़ी च चक्रधारस्तथैव च ॥३५०॥
कल्याणाख्यवराली च मञ्जुभाषा ततः परम् ।
सिंहरवस्तथा रागस्तथैव पटमञ्जरी ॥३५१॥
सर्वे गौलास्तथा नाटाः कल्पतरुस्तथैव च ।
एते रागाः प्रगीयन्ते तृतीयप्रहरोत्तरम् ॥३५२॥
सेंधवो मेघरागश्च मल्लारी पञ्चमस्तथा ।
नीलाम्बरी मुखारी च भैरवी ललितस्तथा ॥३५३॥
मेघनादस्तथा देशी रागो मंगलकोशकः ।
गौडरागश्च मल्लारो रागः आनन्दभैरवी ॥३५४॥
शङ्करानन्दमानव्यौ राजधानी च शर्वरी ।
सावेरीराग इत्येताः सर्वदा च सुखप्रदाः ॥३५५॥

It is Ahobala, who, for the first time gives a very
clear expression about the Rāgas he had actually
dealt with, and the verses quoted from his text are
the evidence for it:

असाधारणधर्मा ये लक्षणत्वेन कीर्तिताः ।
तैरेव रागभेदाः स्युस्तांस्तु वक्ष्येऽत्र कालतः ॥३५६॥
न्यासांशौ यत्र नोच्येते तम षड्जं विदुर्बुधाः ।
आदावुद्गृह्यते येन स तानोद्ग्रहकारकः ॥३५७॥
शुद्धमेलोद्भवः पूर्णो धैवतादिकमूर्छनः ।

Shrinivas Pundit is the author of *Rāga Tatva Vibodha*. It is a small but interesting text on the theory of North Indian music of the first half of the eighteenth century.

He has dealt with the shrutis, Swaras and Murchhnas in the beginning of his book which shows the difference of opinion among the musicians of his time. Then he defines the 'Mela' or 'Thata' and puts it in his own inimitable style. Here is a verse from his text for evidence.

मेल स्वर समूहः स्याद्राग व्यञ्जनशक्तिमान् ।
श्लिष्टोच्चारणमेवात्र समुदायः प्रकीर्तितः ॥

That is, a Mela or Thata is a series of notes or collection of notes—that are capable of producing Rāga. He puts the 'Mela' into three forms namely:

शुद्धैः स्वरेः समस्तैर्यो युक्तः सम्पूर्ण शब्दभाक ।
षड्जिः षाडव इस्युक्तः स्तरै पञ्चभिरौडुवं ॥
एवं मेल स्त्रिधा प्रोक्तो विकृतंश्च स्वरैरिह ।

He means to say that when a 'Mela' takes all the Sudhdha Swara or note it is called 'Sampurna,' when it takes only six notes it is said to be 'Shadava' and when it uses only five notes, it is known as 'Odava.' In the following verses he again enumerates the exact number of possible Rāgas:

शुद्ध सम्पूर्ण मेलस्य भेद एक उदाहृतः ।
तत्वे कैंकस्वरत्यागात् षाडवः षड्विधोमतः
पञ्चाधिकदशतर्वंहि स्वरद्वय वियोगतः ॥

That is, 'Sudhdha-Sampurna' Mela has only one form, with the omission of one note at a time from the 'Mela,' only six varieties are available, if two notes are dropped together fifteen varieties are produced, for example: If *Ni, Dha, Pa, Ma, Ga,* and *Re* is omitted one at a time, then six varieties of Shadava Rāgas are produced. Similarly, when the following pairs of notes are dropped in succession, then only fifteen different forms are available, namely:

Ni-Dha, Ni-Pa, Ni-Ma, Ni-Ga, Ni-Re.
Dha-Pa, Dha-Ma, Dha-Ga, Dha-Re.
Pa-Ma, Pa-Ga, Pa-Re.
Ma-Ga, Ma-Re and Ga-Re.

It has already been accepted by all the previous authors of the medieaval age that a Rāga is derived from the 'Mela or Thata' which, with the omission, of one or two notes at a time, and also with the help of Aroha and Avaroha (ascent and descent) becomes Rāg itself. This is only possible when the system of Sampurna-Shadava and Odava is followed mention of which has been made ere now.

It can be concluded here that through mathematical calculation four hundred and eighty four Rāgs can be derived from the 'Sampurna Mela.' It should be noted here that producing Rāgs from a mela by mathematical calculation as pointed out above is the current principle on which the South Indian, that is, the Karnatic music is based and accepted by all.

Thus it is, that this process laid down by both Ahobala and Shrinivas regarding 'Mela or Thata' which is only a series of notes produces Rāgas. A sloka verse from their works will suffice to illustrate:

मेल स्तर समूहः स्याद्राग्गव्यञ्जनशक्तिमान् ।

The function of 'Mela' is only to put the right notes with the exact 'Varjya-Avarjya' rule for the Rāga intended to be sung, where as the Murchanas added

the requirement of 'Aroha' and 'Avaroha,' thus Rāgas
are produced. In the present system of music which
is commonly known as the Hindusthani Sangeet Padh-
ati the term Murchhana has lost all the ancient or
medieaval significance. The Murchanas coinciding
with the Mela becomes undistinguishable from it.
That the Mela directly produces 'Rāga' by the process of 'Aroha' and 'Avaroha,' can be strongly asserted
as some of the Mahomedan professional artists are
known to use the term in the sense of a kind of
'Gamaka.' In the Southern music system even now,
'Murchhanas' merely mean the 'Aroha' and 'Avaroha'
and nothing else.

It can be said here obviously that the music of
India in the medieaval age was in a flourishing state.
The scholars of that age, leaving aside the old legends,
which were full of controversies, introduced so many
new things and added to the then current music of
the country; and that very system has been followed
by the modern scholars.

Ahobala Shrinivas and Hridaryanarayan located
the actual place of each note both sharp and flat of
the octave, by means of measuring the wire of the
Veena—the popular and most common stringed instru-
ment of those days. This process has made the works
of these authors very valuable to us to fix the different
notes used in different Rāgas of those days. Also the
system of 'Mela' or 'Thata,' classification of 'Rāgs,'
'Rāg Lakshna' and the exact number of Rāgs through
calculation is worth appreciation.

Every one of the above mentioned scholars has
offered unique ideas of his own—which has enriched
the literature of music of the medieaval age. Not only
the theory but also the practical side of this art had

reached its zenith. That is why most of the historians say that the art of music had reached its climax during the reign of the Moguls, mainly, under the patronage and Royal support of the great Emperor Akbar 1556 AD to 1605 AD. During this long period of six hundred years many new Rāgs which were chiefly borrowed from the music of Persia, Arabia, Syria and Messopotamia were introduced and then assimilated with the music of India.

Various types of songs in different rhythms or Tala such as 'Dhrupada,' 'Dhamar,' or 'Hori,' 'Kheyal,' 'Tarana,' 'Chaturanga,' 'Bhajan' etc., were introduced by the great musicians of the by-gone age. The current music of these days i.e., 'Hindusthani music' is a beautiful monument of the fusion of Hindu and Islamic culture of the medieaval age.

Many Rāgas were introduced by Amir Khusru when he was attached to the court of Allauddin Khilji. Raja Man Singh of Gwalior, Sultan Husain Shirqui of Jaunpur, Mahomed Shah, Mira Bai, Tulsi Das and Sur Das were the creators of different types of songs and melodies that are still sung at present by the lovers of music.

Miyan Tan Sen is said to hold the highest position in the sphere of music and commanded an unchallenged reputation and respect for his exhaustive knowledge. Rāgas namely 'Miyan-ki-Maller,' 'Darabari Kanada,' 'Miyan-ki-Saranga' etc., are the bright examples of his masterly compositions. These Rāgas are so sweet that they became very popular and are sung even today by the experts of the present age.

It has been told already that in Ancient India 'Jati Gayana' was in vogue and 'Rāg Gayana' was introduced by the scholars of the medieaval age—which was altogether a new thing to the foreigners. Through long perseverance they were able to assimilate the music both of the east and west and gave an unique shape to it which is current at present.

Ill. 6. Kāmod Rāginī. Deccan, 18th century.

The Origin of Rāga

Pundit Vishnu Narayan Bhatkhande—whose monumental works on the system of present day music have removed all dissensions and placed before the music-loving people the whole theory of this art in a very lucid way based on scientific lines. One of his works in Sanskrit entitled *Lakshya Sangeet* deals entirely with the theory of music. This is the only work which we possess, that answers almost all the queries that may arise in the mind of a beginner, an advanced student and also the person, who, is misled by such, who, himself possesses only a smattering knowledge of the subject.

He has accepted the system expounded by his predecessors of the medieaval age and puts them in a more easy, scientific and reasonable way. He begins with the following verses:

रागास्तावद्दशविधा भरताद्यैरुदीरिताः ।
ग्राम रागा श्चोप रागा रागा भाषाविभाषिकाः ॥
तथैवान्तर भाषाख्या रागांगाख्यास्ततः परम् ।
भाषांगानि क्रियांगानि चोपांगानि पुनः क्रमात ॥
दशस्वेतेषु रागेषु ग्रामरागादयः पुनः ।
रागास्त्वन्तरभाषान्ता मार्गरागा भवन्ति षट् ॥

ततो गंधर्वलोकेन प्रजोज्यास्ते व्यवस्थिताः ।
तस्माद्रागांगभीषांगक्रियांगोपांग संज्ञिकाः ॥
रागाश्चत्वार एवैते देशिरागाः प्रकीर्तिताः ॥
रागांगादिचतुष्कं तु सांप्रतं स्यात्सुगोचरम् ।
संगीते दाक्षिणात्यानामिति सर्वत्र संमतम् ॥
मूर्छनाया रहस्यं तद्रत्नाकरप्रपंचितम् ।
स्फुटमेवाभवद्गोढुं न शक्तः कोऽपि पण्डितः ॥
जातिप्रकरणं चापि रत्नाकरनिरूपितम् ।
अनेकानुकृतं सद्यो ज्ञातुं शक्तो न कोऽपि तत् ॥

In these verses Pt. Bhatkhande refers to the ancient
system of Grama—Murchhanas and Jatis and the ten
types of Rāgas deploring the impossibility of explain-
ing them to-day (a detailed account of them has
already been made in the first two chapters of this
text).

After describing the theory of 'nāda' i.e., sound
in details the author takes up the actual notes that
are used practically both in vocal and instrumental
music, and keeps aside the remaining ten 'Shrutis' or
microtonal intervals of sound—practical use of which
entirely depends upon the skillfulness of the best
artists.

He had accepted the seven sudhdha—and five
vikritas—notes in an octave. The following verses
quoted from his text explain the idea of the great
scholar:

हिन्दुस्थानीयपद्धत्यां लक्ष्यलक्षणकोविदैः ।
सप्त शुद्धास्तथा पञ्च विकृता निश्चिताः स्वराः ॥३६॥
संज्ञास्तेषामथो वच्मि लक्ष्यसङ्गीतगोचराः ।
यतः स्याद्रागनिर्देशे सर्वेषां सुखबोधनम् ॥३७॥
शुद्धाः सप्त स्वराः शुद्धपूर्वया तत्तदाख्यया ।
विज्ञेयाः क्रमशः शुद्धषड्जः शुद्धर्षभस्ततः ॥३८॥

शुद्धगान्धार इत्युक्तः शुद्धमध्यम इत्यपि ।
शुद्धपञ्चम इत्येवं शुद्धधैवत इत्यपि ॥
ततः शुद्धनिषादश्चेत्येवं सप्त स्वराभिधाः ॥३६॥
विकृताः पञ्च कथ्यंते प्रथमः कोमलर्षभः ।
द्वितीयः कोमलो गः स्यात्तृतीयस्तीव्रमध्यमः ॥४०॥
चतुर्थः कोमलो धाख्यः पञ्चमः कोमलाख्यनिः ।
आहत्य शुद्धविकृताः स्वरा द्वादश ईरिताः ॥४१॥

(लक्ष्यसंगीत पृष्ठ ५०)

He says that when, out of these twelve degrees of
the Complete Gamat, one variety each of the 'Chalas-
wara' with all the 'Achala Swaras' fixed note arran-
ged in their proper order, lowest to the highest form
a Mela or Thata. Thus a large number of different
Melas can be produced by different combinations,
each of which becomes the source of several Rāgas.

Mela or Thata System

मेलः स्वरसमूहः स्याद्रागव्यंजनशक्तिमान् ।
श्लिष्टोच्चारणमेवात्र समूहः परिकीर्तितः ॥

A 'Mela,' 'Thata' or parent scale is a series of seven
notes taken in their order beginning from 'Sa' the key-
note of the octave. That is, such combination of notes
which produces 'Rāgas' immediately it is sung or
played is known as 'Mela' or 'Thata.' The important
points regarding the same may be noted below for a
proper attention and consideration that it deserves.

1. What is the main significance and utility of the
twelve notes that are contained in an octave?

2. How many 'Melas' are derived out of the twelve
notes that are contained in an octave?

3. How many 'Melas' are in practical use for the
classification of the current Rāgas?

It was Lochana—who, after a minute observation of the then current system of 'Rāga' and 'Rāginis' of his own time—realised that the Rāga-Rāgini system was fantastic and absolutely untenable. So he adopted the system of 'Mela' which was already prevalent in the South having been, for the first time introduced by Ramamatya, author of *Swara Mela Kalanidhi*. Lochana found this system of Rāga classification to be more proper and helpful to the students of music, an easy and scientific method for the beginners, as well as for such persons, who had some knowledge of the same. Therefore, the system of 'Mela' introduced by him, proved to be more useful and important as it is easy to understand and easier to follow. That is why all his successors followed this system without the least objection.

Till the end of the seventeenth century AD, there was a great difference of opinion, no doubt, regarding the exact number of 'Melas' that could be obtained out of the twelve notes that are contained in the octave.

Current Melas and Rāgas derived from them

A South Indian Pundit named Vyankata Mukhi placed before all interested people, the exact number of 'Melas' which he had calculated mathematically.

In his opinion only seventy two 'Melas' can be derived from the twelve notes of the octave. An objection may be raised here that the author was a compiler of music text on the Southern system and not of the North, but it can be easily answered that the basic principles, such as, 'Mela' and 'Rāga' formation are common to both the systems. Therefore the proposition laid down by him, which is, absolu-

tely based on strictly mathematical calculation may
safely be applied to both the systems equally well.
He was so confident about his own research, that he
says with certainty, that the number of 'Melas'
worked out by him can neither be increased nor
decreased even by Mahadeva himself the master of
the art of music. viz.

यदि कश्चिन्न दुर्नीतो मेलेभ्यस्तु द्विसप्ततेः ।
न्यूनं वाप्यधिकं वापि प्रसिद्धेर्द्वादशस्वरैः ॥
कल्पयेन्मेलने तर्हिममायासो वृथा भवेत् ।
न हि तत्कल्पने भाललोचनोऽपी प्रगल्भते ॥

It is the opinion of all the authors of music of
these days, that, only seventy two Melas or Thatas
can be derived from the twelve notes of the octave
and only ten out of them, namely, Bilaval, Kalyan,
Khamach, Bhairava, Puravi, Marwa, Kaphi, Asaveri,
Bhairavi and Todi are more important than the rest.
viz.

कल्याणीमेलकस्त्वाद्यो वेलावली द्वितीयकः ।
खमाजाख्यस्तृतीयः स्याद्रूं रवाख्यश्चतुर्थकः ॥
पञ्चमः पूर्विकासंज्ञः षष्ठः स्यान्मारवाभिधः ।
सप्तमः काफिसंज्ञः स्यादासावरी तथाष्टमः ॥
नवमो भैरवी मेलो दशमस्तोडिकाह्वयः ।
इत्येते दशमेलास्ते रागोत्पादनहेतवः ॥

(लक्ष्यसंगीत पृष्ठ ७७)

Majority of the Rāgas of the Hindusthani music
system are derived from the 'Thatas' mentioned above,
because they generate all the current and rare Rāgas
described in the literature of music both of the medieaval and modern age. The basic principles and the
essential conditions of a 'Thata' which every student
of music should know are quoted below:

1. A 'Mela' must have all the seven notes of the octave in order of succession, which is not allowed in a Rāga.

2. Both the forms of a note, such as, sharp and flat may be used one after the other in a 'Thata,' that is not permitted in a Rāga.

3. It is not essential for a 'Thata' to have the qualities of pleasing the listeners, which is essential in a Rāga formation.

Rāga

It is now clear to all, that the function of a 'Thata' is only to produce *Rāga*. This very term stands as an intricate question that very often creates a situation of mere confusion. The term *Rāga* may be defined in various ways. But the root meaning of this word is as follows:

स्वरवर्णं विशेषेण ध्वनिभेदेन वा पुनः ।
रज्यते येन यः कश्चित् स रागः संमतःसताम् ॥

(वृहद्देशी पृष्ठ ८१)

That is a 'Rāga' must be appealing and pleasing to all. Majority of the authors have defined the term *Rāga* thus:

1.

योऽसौ ध्वनिविशेषस्तु स्वरवर्णविभूषितः ।
रंजको जनचित्तानां स च राग उदाहृतः ॥२८१॥

(वृहद्देशी पृष्ठ ८१)

2.

होलावश्चित्तसारः स्याद् रागस्यान्दोलनं भवेत् ।
रक्तिस्वरूपं रागस्य रागच्छाया तदाश्रया ॥६०॥

(संगीतसमय सार पृष्ठ १२)

3.

रंजकः स्वरसंदर्भो राग इत्यभिधीयते ।

(संगीत पारिजात पृष्ठ ३०)

4.

योऽयं ध्वनिविशेषस्तु स्वरवर्णं विभूषितः ।
रंजको जन चित्तानां स रागः कथ्यते बुधैः ॥६६॥

(लक्ष्यसंगीत पृष्ठ ६६)

That is, in short, a Rāga is the combination of different notes that are contained in an octave, with 'Varnas that pleases the listeners. The following are essential *Conditions* for the production of a Rāga.'

Rāga Jati and its Number

1. A 'Rāga' is derived from some 'Thata' and may contain seven, six or at least five notes of the 'Mela' from which it is produced.

औडुवः पंचभिः प्रोक्तः स्वरैः षड्भिश्चषाडवः ।
संपूर्णः सप्तभिर्ज्ञेय एवं रागास्त्रिधा मतः ॥

That is, as a rule a 'Sampurna Rāga' must have all the seven notes of the octave, whereas a 'Shadava Rāga' takes any six and an 'Odava Rāga' uses only five notes that are contained in an octave, except that the notes 'Ma' and 'Pa' are never dropped both together at the same time.

Thus by mere mathematical calculation the total number of Rāgas that can be produced from one single Thata by the Varya-avarya process comes to Four hundred eighty four. If all the seventy two Thatas of Pt. Vyankata Mukhi are accepted then 34834 Rāgas are obtained, for example:

Rāga Jati		Exact Number
1. Sampurna-Sampurna	Rāga	1
2. ,, Shadava	Rāga	6
3. ,, Odava	Rāga	15
4. Shadava Sampurna	Rāga	6

5.	,,	Shadava.	Rāga	36
6.	,,	Odava	Rāga	90
7.	Odava-Sampurna.		Rāga	15
8.	,,	Shadava.	,,	90
9.	,,	Odava.	,,	225

Total Number of Rāgas 484

पूर्णारोहावरोहः स्यात् प्रकारस्त्वेक एव हि ।
सम्पूर्णषाडवास्तत्र षडेव संभवंति ते ॥३८॥
संपूर्णाडुवकाश्चाथ पंचदशमिता मताः ।
इति परिस्फुटं भूयादनायासेन तद्विदाम् ॥३६॥
षाडवारोहसंपन्ना विलोमे षाडवाः पुनः ।
षट्त्रिंशद्रूदकास्तत्र मन्यन्ते लक्ष्यकोविदैः ॥४०॥
षाडवौडुवभेदास्ते नवतिः संप्रकीर्तिताः ।
पंचदशहताः षट् ते परिस्फुटं विवेकिनाम् ॥४१॥
औडुवारोहसंपन्नाः संपूर्णा अवरोहणे ।
पंच दश प्रकारास्ते संभवेयुर्मते विदाम ॥४२॥
औडुवारोहसंयुक्ता विलोमे षाडवास्तथा ।
नवति प्रतिमा भेदाः सर्वलक्ष्यज्ञसंमताः ॥४३॥
औडुवौडुवभेदास्ते शरनेत्रकराः स्मृताः ।

(लक्ष्यसंगीत पृष्ठ ६२)

2. If both the forms of the same note, flat and
sharp, occur in a Rāga—which however happens rarely
—it is as a rule that the sharp notes are usually used
in ascending and the flat notes are used while descending, in such a Rāga in which both the forms of a
note are used, but there are exceptions.

Almost all the twelve notes of the octave i.e. sharp
and flat have now come to use in the Rāgas Bhairavi
and Pilu. It is allowed in these two Rāgas only under
the rules of 'रंजको जनचित्तानां स रागः कथ्यते बुधैः' i.e. the effect
of a Rāga must be pleasing to the ear. These two
Rāgas are considered to be the most popular and

Ill. 7. Megha Malhār Rāga. Rajput Miniature, Amber, AD 1709.

common among those, even who, do not know any
thing about music. People like the bullockcart drivers
and the Tongavalas of the Uttar Pradesh usually sing
these two Rāgas when they are in mood.

Both the Madhyamas are used in 'Lalit' just one
after the other. It is permitted in this Rāga, only
because, without the use of both the Madayamas, the
Rāga cannot be recognized and it will also remain
undeveloped. The main characteristic of this Rāga
depends upon the Madhyamas.

The other forms of the same notes are usually used
in a Rāga as a 'Vivadi' note, i.e. to beautify the Rāga.
The following verse is an excellent analogy regarding
the same given by the modern scholars of music:

विवादिनं स्वरं प्रायो योजयन्त्वरोहणे ।
न तच्छास्त्वेऽतिदोषाईमित्यूचुर्लक्ष्यवेदिनः ॥
सुप्रमाण्युतो मन्ये विवादयपि सुरक्तिदः ।
यथेषत्कृष्णावर्णेन शुभ्रस्यातिविचित्रता ॥

(लक्ष्यसंगीत पृष्ठ ७४)

3. A Rāga must have the 'Vernas' that is ascent
and descent.

गानक्रियोच्यते वर्णः स चतुर्घनिरुपितः ।
स्थाय्यारोह्यवरोही च संचारीत्यथलक्षणम् ॥

(लक्ष्यसंगीत पृष्ठ ६७)

That is four kinds of 'varnas' namely 'asthaiee,'
'arohi,' 'avarohi' and 'sanchari' are used when a rāga
is practically sung or played. The function of all these
afore-said 'varnas' is so important in the development
of a Rāga that without these a rāga cannot be sung
properly and well. Besides these there are four kinds
of 'swaras' more generally known as 'vadi,' 'samavadi,' 'vivadi' and 'anuvadi.'

चतुर्विधाः स्वरा वादी संवादी च विवाद्यपि ।
अनुवादी च वादी तु प्रयोगे बहुलस्वरः ॥

(लक्ष्यसंगीत पृष्ठ ७१)

That is, the 'Vadi' note is just like the king or main
note in the Rāga, whereas the 'Samavadi' note is just
like the minister to the king, so to say the next in
importance to the 'Vadi' note. The 'Vivadi' is the
enemy note, because when it is used in any Rāga im-
properly it produces a discordant sound or destroys
the harmony of the Rāga. The note 'Anuvadi' is just
like the servant or follower without any importance
of his own.

The notes namely 'Vadi' and 'Samavadi' are very
important in a Rāga because they discharge two main
functions. Firstly they determine the identity of the
Rāga and also the class of the same and, secondly, the
time when it is to be sung or played.

Now the author quotes the signs (Lakshana) through
which a Rāga is to be judged and recognised. It refers
to the ancient system of development, and does not
apply to the music of the Lakshya-Sangeet. It is an
evidence to show how systematic the Rāga development used to be in ancient music and it would better,
if, some such rules were formed for the Rāga development of the current system of music.

Rāga Gayana

रंजयन्ति मनांसीति रागास्ते दशलक्षणाः ।
लक्षणानि दशोक्तानिलक्ष्यन्ते तावदादितः ॥
ग्रहांशौ मंद्रतारौ च न्यासापन्यासकौ तथा ॥
अथ संन्यासविन्यासौ बहुत्वं चाल्पता तथा ।
लक्षणानि दशैतानि रागाणां मुनयोऽब्रुवन् ॥

(चतुर्दंडिप्रकाश)

The scholar has also mentioned the points regarding a Rāga through which it is to be identified, namely, 'Graha,' 'Amsa,' 'Mandra,' 'Tara,' 'Nayasa,' 'Apanyas,' 'Sanyas,' 'Binyas,' 'Bahuttva Alpattva.' If all these points be compared with those given in the rules of 'Jati-Gayana,' it can be ascertained here that the above said rules regarding the Rāga are chiefly borrowed from those ascribed to 'Jati-Gayana' of the ancient times. It is also probable that, when, 'Rāga-Gayana' came in force all these rules that were essential for the fulfilment of the 'Jati-Gayana' were attached to *Rāga-Gayana.*

ग्रहांशतारमंद्राश्च न्यासापन्यासकौ तथा ।
अपि सन्यासविन्यासौ बहुत्वं चाल्पता ततः ।।
एतान्यंतरमार्गेण सह लक्ष्माणि जातिषु ।
षाडवौडुविते क्वापीत्येव माहुस्त्रयोदश ।।

Majority of the ancient scholars say that 'Rāga-Gayana' is the fourth type of current geetas or songs of those days chiefly derived from 'Jati-Gayana.' The following statement from Brihaddesi supports the same:

इदानीं सम्प्रवक्ष्यामि सप्त गितीर्मनोहराः ।
प्रथमा शुद्धगितीस्याद् द्वितीया भिन्नका भवेत् ।।
तृतीया गौडिका चैव रागगीतिश्चतुर्थिका ।
साधारणी तु विज्ञेया गीतिज्ञैः पञ्चमी तथा ।।
भाषागीतिस्तुषष्ठी स्पाद विभाषा चैव सप्तमी ।
सप्तगीत्यो मया प्रोक्ता इदानीं भेद उच्यते ।।

It is now evident, that the mode of singing the Rāgas, is mainly derived from the ancient 'Jati-Gayana,' which is in due course of time blended with the music of Persia, Arabia, Syria, and Mesopotamia.

Late Sangeetacharya Pundit Vadi lal Shivaram of

Ahmedabad, one of the best and leading scholars of
music, who, was considered to be the living encyclo-
paedia of the literature of music says, that, if the present Rāgas are sung properly then it is the most difficult task even for the top-most artists of these days to
sing any Rāga more than a couple of minutes. But he
firmly believes that the purity of Rāgas as they are
in the present form should be very strictly followed
by every student of music. The following verses quoted
from Chaturdandi Prakasika will give the exact sense
of 'Rāga-Lakshana':

रंजयन्ति मनांसीति रागास्ते दशलक्षणाः ।
लक्षणानि दशोक्तानि लक्ष्यन्ते तावदादितः ॥
ग्रहाशौ मन्द्रतारौ च न्यासापन्यासकौ तथा ।
अथ सन्यासविन्यासौ बहुत्वं चाल्पता तथा ॥
लक्षणानि दशैतानि रागाणां मुनयोऽब्रुवन् ॥

A common rule that was always followed by both
the ancient and medieaval artists, is that, they had to
begin the 'Geeta' that is song from a particular note,
which is known as 'Graha' and they had also to make
an end of the song on a definite note named 'Nyasa.'
The prominent note in the song is said to be 'Amsa
Swara.' The proper use of the former two notes is
not in common practice but the present 'Vadi' note
is the modified form of the 'Amsa Swara' of the by-
gone age. For example:

गीतं प्रारभ्यते येन सस्वरो ग्रह ईरितः ।
गीतसमाप्तिकृत्र्यासो वर्ण्यते चांशकोऽध्नुा ॥
बहुशो गीयते येन स्वरेणांशः स कथ्यते ।
अंश स्वरस्त्वसावेव जीवस्वर इति स्मृतः ॥
अधुना लक्ष्यमार्गे तु मेलजात्यादि साधनैः ।
तथा वादिस्वरेणैव सर्वे रागाः सुवर्णिता : ॥

Regarding the term 'Mandra' and 'Tara' they are in the rising order of pitch known as 'Mandra, Madhya and Tara' Sthana. But the words namely 'Apanyas,' 'Sanyas,' 'Binyas,' 'Bahuttva' and 'Alpattva' are purely technical terms absolutely meant for the higher students for their higher studies in music. So these terms can safely be avoided here undiscussed—as they are not much connected with the topics of the present work. Moreover these terms have become obsolete now-a-days.

Now let us look at the time-table of Rāgas that is the rules showing the proper times at which different Rāgas are to be sung or played. It cannot be denied that each Rāga has its own emotion or feeling and also mood or passion. In order to encourage the same and also to have the full advantage of it the artists are habituated to sing a particular Rāga at a specific hour of the day or night. Narada the author of Sangeet Makaranda has considered that one who sings and also those who hear music untimely not only destroy the beauty or harmony of the Rāga but also lose their longevity.

For the purpose of determining the times of singing, Rāgas have been classified into three groups according to the notes used in them, for example:

1. 'Sandhi Prakash Rāgas.' 2. 'Purva or Purvanga Vadi Rāgas' and 3. 'Utter or Uttaranga Vadi Rāgas.'

Sandhi Prakash Rāgas are such, as are usually sung or played at twilight that is just an hour before and after the sunrise and sunset, *i.e.*, between 5 a.m. to 7 a.m. and 5 p.m. to 7 p.m. The characteristic of these Rāgas is entirely based upon the notes used in them, for intance: 'Komala Risava' flat D is essential, both forms of 'Madhyama' that is flat and sharp F may be used either separately, simultaneously or just one after the other and the other notes are all Sudhdha—sharp. Here is a beautiful quotation from *Lakshya Sangeet* page 74 that gives an exact idea of it.

प्रातःकाले तथा सायंकाले गेयास्तु ये मताः ।
संधिप्रकाशनामानो रागा अस्माभिरीरिताः ॥
एतद्रागेषु निर्दिष्टं वैचित्र्यं लक्ष्यवेदिभिः ।
मृदुत्वं रिधयोश्चाथ तीव्रत्वं गनिषादयोः ॥
सायंकालप्रगेयत्वं तीव्रमेण भवेत्स्फुटम् ।
शुद्धमेन भवेतद्वत् प्रातःकालप्रसूचनम् ॥

Pundit Bhatkhande says that among these Sandhi-Prakash Rāgas 'Tivra Madhyama' if prominent, denotes evening twilight whereas the prominence of Shuddha Madhyama indicates morning twilight. That is the prominence of 'Madhyama' denotes the time and nothing else.

The Rāgas derived from Bhairava, Purvi and Marva Mela or Thata can be placed in this group.

Purva Rāga—Rāgas that are sung after 'Sandhi Prakash Rāgas' and before the mid-night and also mid-day are said to be the 'Purva or Purvanga Vadi Rāga.' That is the 'Vadi' or predominent note of these Rāgas are always found in any of the notes viz., 'Sa,' 'Re,' 'Ga,' 'Ma' or 'Pa.' It is sung between 7 a.m. and mid-day and 7 p.m. to midnight. The Rāgas derived from Bilaval, Kalyan and Khamach mela or thata which take all the Sudhdha or sharp notes of the octave and also Tivra Madhyama in the case of Kalyan and Komal Nishada, which is permitted, can be placed in this group, in the case of Vilabal Kalyan, and Khamach respectively.

Rāgas with komal Gandhara and Nishada and also Rishava and Dhaivata in both the forms are

known as Utter or Uttaranga Vadi Rāga. These
Rāgas are sung after the 'Purva Rāgas' and before
the 'Sandhi Prakash Rāgas,' say between mid-day to
4 or 5 p.m. and also between midnight to 4 or 5 a.m.
The Vadi notes of all these Rāgas generally stick to
any one note of the second half of the octave that is
'Pa,' 'Dha,' 'Ni,' and top 'Sa.' Rāgas derived from
Kafi, Asaveri, Bhairavi and Todi are considered to
belong to this group.

The following quotations from *Abhinava Rāga
Manjari'* will give a clear idea of it:

स्वरविकृतयधीनाः स्युस्त्रयो वर्गा व्यवस्थिताः ।
रागाणामिह मर्मज्ञैर्गानिसौकर्यहेतवे ॥
रिगधतीव्रका रागा वर्गोग्रिमे व्यवस्थिताः ।
संधिप्रकाशनामानः क्षिप्ता वर्गे द्वितीयके ॥
तृतीये निहताः सर्वे गनिकोमल मण्डिताः ।
व्यवस्थेयं समीचीना गानकालविनिर्णये ॥
प्रातर्गेयास्तथा सायं गेया रागाः संततत् ।
संधिप्रकाशवर्गं स्युरिति सर्वत्र संमतम् ॥
ततः परं समादिष्टं गानं लक्ष्यानुसारतः ।
रिगधतीव्रकाणां तद्रागाणां भूरिरक्षितदम् ॥
गनिकोमलसम्पन्ना रागा गीता विशेषतः ।
मध्याह्ने च तथा मध्याराव्ने संगीतविन्मते ॥

It is to be noted here that, the two main classes
Poorva and Utter Rāgas are formed from the Vadi
and Samavadi aspect and not exactly from the flat
and sharp note point of view.

Poorva Rāga, Rāgas having their Vadi in Poor-
vang are sung during 12 noon to mid-night. Similarly
Utter or Utteranga Rāgas having their Vadi note in
Utteranga are sung between mid-night and mid-day.
These Rāgas may be classified into the following two
groups according to the notes used as Vadi in them.

Group I

Poorva Rāgas:

    (a) Vadi in Poorvanga

    (b) Time during 12 noon and mid-night.

Utter Rāgas:

    (a) Vadi in Utteranga

    (b) Time between mid-night to mid-day i.e., 12 noon to mid-night.

The notes namely 'सा', 'म' and 'प' (C, F & G) appear in both the Angas, therefore Rāgas having any one of them as Vadi are some of them, Poorva Rāgas and some other Utter Rāgas.

Group II

According to 'Swaras' notes 'Sudhdha' and 'Vikirta' flat and sharp.

1. (a) Sandhi Prakash—both morning and evening 'Swaras' required 'Komal Rishava' and 'Tivra Gandhara' (Flat 'D' and Sharp 'E.')

(b) Madhyama, if 'Tivra' sharp alone or more prominent where both the Madhyamas occur, denotes evening twilight. For example, Pooravi, Shree, Puriya-Dhanashree and Gouri. If Suddha Madhyama occurs alone or more prominent where both the Madhyamas are used the Rāgas belong to morning twilight group. For example, Bhairava, Ramkali, Lalit and Kalingda.

Students are advised to note that the prominence of 'Tivra Madhyama' F sharp in any group denotes night time or evening twilight and 'Suddha Madhyama' Flat 'F' denotes morning time or morning twilight. For example the Rāgas, namely, Basant, Paraj, Lalit, Sohini, Kalingda, Bhairava and Ramkali are sung between 3 a.m. to 9 a.m. whereas the Rāgas

Ill. 8. Śrī Rāga. Rajput Miniature, Amber, AD 1709.

Shree, Puravi, Puriya-Dhanashree, and Marava, are sung in the 4th quarter of the day.

2. Rāgas having 'Tivra' (shuddha) 'Re' and Shuddha 'Dha' are usually sung in the first quarter of the day and night subject to the above mentioned rule about Madhyamas.

3. Rāgas having 'Komal' Ga and 'Komal' Ni are to be sung during the second and third quarters of the day and night according to the 'Angas' subject to the rule about 'Tivra Madhyama' F sharp.

In the description of a Rāga the following points should be remembered and followed by every student of music, because it fulfills almost all conditions required for the same, described by the modern scholars:

1. The name of the 'Mela' or 'Thata' from which a Rāga is derived should be mentioned i.e., the name of the parent scale of the Rāga is required.

2. A detailed account of all the notes that are used or omitted in a Rāga in its ascent or descent or in both be given i.e., the 'Aroha' ascent and 'Avaroha' descent of the same be given.

3. It is essential to mention the 'Jati' of the Rāga i.e. 'Sampurna,' 'Shadava' or 'Odava' is required.

4. Time of singing of the Rāgas and the class to which it belongs accordingly should be mentioned.

5. The following 'Swaras' namely 'Vadi,' 'Samavadi,' 'Vivadi' if any, and 'Anuvadi' are essential in the description of each Rāga.

6. Characteristic or identifying passages that is 'पकड़' of each Rāga are needed. A detailed description of all the ten principal Rāgas is given below with reference to the Sanskrit texts of the modern scholars:

1. Rāga Yaman:

   a. Rāga Yaman is derived from Kalyan Mela

b. Ascent. Sa. Re. Ga. Madhyama Tivra Pa.
Dha. Ni. Sa. Descent. Sa. Ni. Dha. Pa. Ma.
Ga. Re. Sa.

c. Vadi 'Ga,' Samavadi 'Ni,' Vivadi sudhdha
Madhyama and the remaining notes are 'Anuvadi.'

d. The Jati of the Rāga is Sampurna.

e. Purva or Purvanga Vadi Rāga.

f. It is sung in the evening that is between 6
p.m. to 9 p.m.

g. The catch notes of this Rāga are, 'Ga Re—,
Ni, Re Sa.'

कल्याण मेल संजात इमनो लोक विश्रुतः ।
गनिसंवादसंपन्न आद्यायामोचितो निशि ॥
केचित्संनिर्दिशन्त्येनं पारसीकप्रदेशजम् ।
अन्येऽस्मद्देशजं प्राहुर्बुधैः कार्योऽत्र निर्णयः ॥
ईषत्स्पर्शेन शुद्धाख्यमध्यमस्य विलोमके ।
कल्याणो यमनाद्योऽसौ जायते तद्विदां मते ॥

2. Rāga Vilabal:

a. Rāga Vilabal is derived from Vilabal Mela.

b. Ascent:—Sa Re Ga ma Pa Dha Ni Sa.
Descent:—Sa Ni Dha Pa ma Ga Re Sa.

c. The Jati of this Rāga is Sampurna-Sampurna.

d. It is an Uttar or Uttaranga Vadi Rāga.

e. Vadi 'Dha,' Samavadi 'Ga,' Vivadi 'Ni' flat
and the remaining notes are 'Anuvadi.'

f. This Rāga is sung in the morning i.e., between 6 a.m. to 9 a.m.

g. The catch notes of this Rāga are, 'Ga Pa
Dha—, Ni Sa.'

शंकराभरणे मेले वेलावलीतिनामकः ।
धैवतांशो मतो लक्ष्ये प्रातः कालोचितस्तथा ॥

प्रातःकालीयकल्याणमेनं शंसन्ति केचन ।
अवरोहे गवक्रत्वं कल्याणांगं निवारयेत् ॥
यदायं मध्यमत्यक्तो निवक्रोऽप्यधिरोहणे ।
वेलावलस्तदाल्हैया पूर्वंकः संभवेद्भ्रुशम् ॥
शुद्धवेलावलीरागे मृदुनिस्वरयोजनात् ।
अल्हैया संभवेल्लक्ष्य इति संगीतविन्मतम् ॥

(लक्ष्यसंगीत पृष्ठ ९५)

3. a. Rāga Khamach is derived from 'Khamach Mela.'

   b. Ascent:—Sa Ga ma Pa Dha Ni Sa.
   Descent:—Sa ni Dha Pa ma Ga Re Sa.

   c. The Jati of this Rāga is 'Shadava-Sampurna.'
   'Re' is omitted in ascending.

   d. It is a Purva or Purvanga vadi Rāga.

   e. 'Vadi' Ga Samavadi Tivra Ni and at times Komal Ga is used as Vivadi and the remaining notes are 'Anuvadi.'

   f. This Rāga is sung at night between 9 p.m. to mid-night.

   g. The catch notes of this Rāga are, 'ni' Dha—, ma Pa Dha—, ma Ga—.'

खंमाजमेलकोऽस्माकं कर्णाटसंज्ञितः पुरा ।
दाक्षिणात्यमते चासौ कांभोजीमेल उच्यते ॥
गांधारोऽत्र मतो वादी संवादी निस्वरो भवेत् ।
गानं चास्या भवेदिष्टं द्वितीयप्रहरे निशि ॥

(लक्ष्यसंगीत पृष्ठ १०७)

4. a. Rāga Bhairava is derived from 'Bhairava Mela.'

   b. Ascent:—Sa re Ga ma Pa dha Ni Sa.
   Descent:—Sa Ñi dha Pa ma Ga re Sa.

   c. The Jati of this Rāga is Sampurana-Sampurna.

d. It is a Sandhi 'Prakash Rāga.'

e. Vadi 'dha,' Samavadi 're,' Vivadi Komal 'Ñishada' and the remaining notes are 'Anuvadi.'

f. This Rāga is sung early in the morning, at least one or two hours before and after the sun rise.

g. The catch notes of this Rāga are, 'ma (ma) re Sa.'

भैरवाख्यसुमेलाञ्च जातो भैरवनामकः ।
आरोहे चावरोहेऽपि संपूर्णः सर्वसंमतः ॥
धैवतः संमतो वादी संवादी ऋषभो भवेत् ।
गानमस्य समादिष्टं प्रातः कालेऽतिरक्तिदम् ॥
प्रारोहे ऋषभाल्पत्वं संप्रोक्तं मर्मवेदिभिः ।
आंदोलनं तथैव स्याद्रिधयोरिति संमतम् ॥
सायंकाले तथा प्रोक्तं वैचित्र्यं गनिषादयोः ।
रिधयोस्तत्तथैव स्यात्प्रातःकाले मते सताम् ॥
(लक्ष्यसंगीत पृष्ठ ११४)

5. a. Rāga Purvi is derived from 'Puravi Mela.'

b. Ascent:—Sa re Ga Ma Pa dha Ni Sa.
   Descent:—Sa Ni dha Pa Ma Ga re Sa.

c. The Jati of this Rāga is Sampurna-Sampurna.

d. It is a Sandhi Prakash Rāga.

e. Vadi 'Ga,' Samavadi 'Ni,' and the remaining notes are 'Anuvadi.'

f. It is sung in the evening, at least one or two hours before and after the sun-set.

g. The catch notes of this Rāga are, 'Ni--, Sa re Ga—, re Sa--.'

पूर्वीतिनामके मेले स्यात्पूर्वी सुखदायिनी ।
आरोहे चाबरोहेऽपि संपूर्णैव मता बुधैः ॥
गांधारः संमतो वादी निषादो मंत्रितुल्यकः ।
गानमस्याः समादिष्टं दिनान्तेऽतिमनोहरम् ॥

प्रयोगः शुद्धमस्याऽत्र सह गेन मतो मनाक् ।
अवरोहे न मे भाति रक्तिहानिकरोऽप्यसौ ॥

(लक्ष्यसंगीत पृष्ठ १२२)

6. a. Marva Rāga is derived from 'Marva Mela.'
   b. Ascent:—Sa re Ga Ma Dha Ni Sa.
      Descent:—Sa Ni Dha Ma Ga re Sa.
   c. It is a 'Shadava-Shadava Rāga,' Panchama is omitted from it.
   d. It is a 'Sandhi Prakash Rāga.'
   e. Vadi 'Dha,' Samavadi 're.' The remaining notes are, 'Anuvadi.'
   f. This Rāga is sung in the evening – that is one or two hours before and aftere the sun-set.
   g. The catch notes of this Rāga are, 'Ni re Ga Ma Dha—Ma Ga re—.'

मारवामेलनोत्पन्ना मारवा लक्ष्यविश्रुता ।
आरोहे चावरोहेऽपि पहीना षाडवा मता ॥
ऋषभोऽत्र मतो वादी कैश्चिद्धैवत ईरितः ।
गानं सुनिश्चितं चास्या दिनान्ते बहुरक्तिदम् ॥
सांयगेय स्वरूपेऽस्मिन् घांशत्वं न सुसंगतम् ।
प्राचीनैर्मारवा प्रोक्ता सांशागांशाथवा ध्रुवम् ॥

(लक्ष्यसंगीत पृष्ठ १३१)

7. a. Rāga Kafi is derived from 'Kafi Mela.'
   b. Ascent:—Sa Re ga ma Pa Dha ni Sa.
      Descent:—Śa ni Dha Pa ma ga Re Sa.
   c. The Jati of this Rāga is 'Sampurna-Sampurna.'
   d. It is a Purva or Purvanga Vadi Rāga.
   e. Vadi 'Pa,' Samavadi 'Sa,' Vivadi 'Sudhdha Gandhara or Nishada' and the remaining notes are 'Anuvadi.'
   f. This Rāga is sung at midnight.
   g. The catch notes are, 'ni Pa ga—Re,' or 'Sa

Sa Re Re ga ga ma ma Pa.'

हरप्रियाख्यमेलोऽत्र लक्ष्येऽत्र काफिसंज्ञितः ।
काफीरागस्तदुत्थः स्यादिति लक्ष्यविदां मतम् ॥
पंचमः संमतो वादी संवादी षड्जनामकः ।
केचिद्गांधारमाहुस्ते वादिनं गानकोविदाः ॥
मध्यरात्रोचितो मेलो यथायं गनिकोमलः ।
मध्याह्नाह्स्तथैवासौ को न जानाति मर्मविद् ॥

(लक्ष्यसंगीत पृष्ठ १३६)

8. a. Rāga Asaveri is derived from 'Asaveri Thata.'
    b. Ascent:—Sa Re ma Pa dha Sa.
       Descent:—Sa ni dha Pa ma ga Re Sa.
    c. The Jati of this Rāga is 'Odava Sampurna.'
    d. 'Ga' and 'Ni' are omitted while ascending.
       It is an Uttar or Uttaranga Vadi Rāga.
    e. Vadi 'dha,' Samavadi 'ga,' and the remain-
       ing notes are 'Anuvadi.'
    f. This Rāga is sung in the morning, i.e., bet-
       ween 9 a.m. to 12 noon.
    g. The catch notes of this Rāga are, 'Sa Re ma
       Pa dha Pa.'

ग्रंथेषु भैरवीमेलो यः पुराणैः प्रकीर्तितः ।
स एवासावरीसंज्ञो लक्ष्ये विद्भिः समादृतः ॥
मेलादस्मात्समुत्पन्न आसावरीति नामकः ।
रागो गुणिप्रियश्चाथ प्रारोहे गनिवर्जितः ॥
धैवतोऽत्र मतो वादी संम्वदी गस्वरो भवेत् ।
गानं चास्य समादिष्टं द्वितीयप्रहरे दिने ॥

(लक्ष्यसंगीत पृष्ठ १५६)

9. a. Rāga Bhairavi is derived from 'Bhairavi
       Mela.'
    b. Ascent:—Sa re gā ma Pa dha ni Sa.
       Descent:—Sa ni dha Pa ma ga re Sa.

   c. The Jati of this Rāga is 'Sampurna-Sampurna.'

   d. It is an Uttar or Uttaranga Vadi Rāga.

   e. Vadi 'ma,' 'Pa' or 'dha,' Samavadi 'Sa' or 'ga.' Vivadi Tivra Madhyama and the remaining notes are 'Anuvadi.'

   f. This Rāga is sung in the morning, between 9 a.m. to 12 noon.

   g. The catch notes are 'ga—, Sa re Sa,' or 'dha—ni Sa re ga—, Sa re Sa.'

> ग्रंथोक्ततोडिकामेलो लक्ष्येऽत्र भैरवीरितः ।
> अस्मान्मेलात्समुत्पन्ना भैरवी लोकविश्रुता ॥
> धैवतः संमतो वादी कंश्चिन्मध्यम ईरितः ।
> आरोहे चावरोहेऽपि सम्पूर्णा सरला मता ॥

(लक्ष्यसंगीत पृष्ठ १३५)

10. a. Todi Rāga is derived from 'Todi Mela.'

   b. Ascent:—Sa re ga Ma Pa dha Ni Sa.
     Descent:—Sa Ni dha Pa Ma ga re Sa.

   c. The Jati of this Rāga is 'Sampurna-Sampurna.'

   d. This is an Uttar or Uttaranga Vadi Rāga.

   e. Vadi 'dha', Samavadi 'ga.' The remaining notes are 'Anuvadi.'

   f. This Rāga is sung in the morning that is some time between 9 a.m. to 12 noon.

   g. The catch notes of this Rāga are, 'dha Ni Sa re ga—re ga —, re Sa.'

> वराटीतोडिकामेलो यो ग्रंथेषु निरूपितः ।
> समादृतः स एवात्र तोडीति लक्ष्यवेदिभिः ॥
> अस्मान्मेलात्समुत्पन्ना रागिणी तोडिका ह्वया ।
> आरोहे चावरोहे च सम्पूर्णा लोकविश्रुता ॥
> धैवतः संमतो वादी गांधारो मंत्रितुल्यकः ।
> गानमस्याः समीचीनं द्वितीय प्रहरेऽहनि ॥

(लक्ष्यसंगीत पृष्ठ १६७)

Appendix

Geeta is a combination of notes that is pleasing to the mind. It is of two kinds:—Gandharva and Gana.

रंजकः स्वरसंदर्भो गीतमित्यभिधीयते ।
गांधर्वं गानमित्यस्य भेदद्वयमुदीरितम् ॥

Gandharva is that music which, like the Vedas did not originate from man and was sung by the Gandharvas and which always aimed at the attainment of 'Moksha,' that is, salvation.

अनादि संप्रदायं यद्गंधर्वैः संप्रयुज्यते ।
नियतं श्रेयसो हेतुस्तद्गांधर्वं जगुर्बुधाः ॥

While the music which was created and systematised by the learned men, and which was used in Deshi Rāgas after being classified, and which aims at pleasing mankind—such music is Gana.

यत्तु वाग्गेय कारेण रचितं लक्षणान्वितम् ।
देशी रागादिषु प्रोक्तम् तद्गानं जनरंजनम् ॥

The commentator of Ratnakar; Kallinath identifies Gandharva and Gana with Marga and Desi sangeet respectively. Because two different names have been used for the same thing. Marga is an obsolete form of music and so needs no place here.

Desi sangeet was in use even in the time of Sharanga Deva, but the said music of his time was altogether a different form that of to-day.

It is known to all that Desi sangeet is variable. As it aims at pleasing the listeners, it always changes with the general taste of the people of all times and places.

देशे देशे जनानं यद्रुच्याहृदयरंजकम् ।
गानं च वादनं नृत्यं तद्देशीत्यभिधीयते ॥

In the days of Saranga Deva, Dhrupada Kheyal, and other such forms of music were not in practical use. Prabhand, Rupaka and Vastu etc., were sung. Prabhand has many parts which were known as Dhatus. The names of these Dhatus are given in Ratnakar and as follows: - Udgraha, Milapak, Dhruva, Antara and Abhog. Now-a-days Prabhandas are not sung any where so we shall not deal with these ancient Dhatus. These Dhatus are similar to those of our present parts of music namely: —Sthaie, Antara, Sanchari and Abhog. Numerous examples of Prabhandas are given in Ratnakar and it is clear that those types of songs are included in the Nibadha Gayana. Sharanga Deva mentions Alaptigana as a part of Anibaddhagana, and it may be called an Aalap.

Some slight difference is there between Alapti and Aalap, though both are the examples of Anibaddhagana.

निवद्धमनिवद्धं तद्द्वेधा निगदितं बुधैः ।
बद्धं धातुभिरंगैश्च निवद्धमभिधीयते ॥
आलप्तिबंधहीनत्वाद निबद्धमितीरितम् ।

The exposition in which the ten essentials of a Rāga —Graha, Amsa, Mandra, Tara, Nyas, Apanyas, Alpatva, Bahutva, Shadavatva and Oudavatva are clearly manifested is known as Ragalap.

प्रहांशमंद्रतारार्णां   न्यासापन्यासयोस्तथा   ।
अल्पत्वस्य   बहुत्वस्य   षाडवौडुवयोरपि   ॥
अभिव्यक्तिर्यत्न दृष्ठा स रागालाप उच्यते ।

It is evident that a singer has to put before the audience all these essentials of a Rāga by which a Rāga could easily be recognised and which have been mentioned by the ancient and medieval authors. The words:—Graha, Amsha, Nyas, Shadvatva, and Auduvatva have been explained before.

Mandra and Tara indicates the limits in the octave of the Rāga. In ancient days there were rules that a Rāga could go down upto a certain note in the Mandra Saptak and rise to a certain pitch in the Tara sthana of the octave.

Apanyas, Sanyas and Vinyas were the cadences or pauses occurring in the course of a song and they were generally known as Vidari. The Dhatus of a Geeta fall in the Vidari class. Later, however, Sanyas and Vinyas were included in Apanyas. So that is why Apanyas has to be very clearly demonstrated in the full development of a Rāga.

Alpatva and Bahutva are not to be related with the Shadavatva and Oudavatva. The latter were connected with the Rāga Mela that is with notes permissible in a Rāga.

Bahutva of a note in a Rāga can be manifested in two ways. One by Alanghan and the other by Abhyas Alanghana is the denial of 'Langhana' (omission), and where the Langhana of a note was to be shown in a Rāga. The slightest use of a note by giving it the least importance by using or at an insignificant place to it. Abhyas means the repetition of a note which could be done in two ways:—1. By repeating the same note consecutively or 2. By using it at intervals, other notes coming in between. This 'Bahutva' has only been given to the 'Vadi' and 'Samavadi' notes of a Rāga. If the 'Bahutva' has to be given to any other note of a Rāga it could be done only with the Puryaya—Amsa note, or a note which was made 'Vadi,' for the time being 'Alanghana,' therefore, of a note means its use in a Rāga in a very insignificant position, when such a note is, ordinarily, to be omitted from the Rāga.

अलंधनात्तथाऽभ्यासाद्बहुत्वं द्विविधं मतम् ।
पर्यायांशे स्थितं तच्च वादिसंवादिनोरपि ॥

'Alpatva' can be explained in two ways:—(1) By 'langhana' and (2) 'Anabhyas.' The meaning of Langhana and Abhyas has been explained before, so we need not deal with the same here again.

अल्पत्वं च द्विधा प्रोक्तमनभ्यासाच्च लंघनात् ।
अनभ्यासस्त्वनंशेषु ' प्रायो लोप्येष्वपीष्यते ॥

It should be noted however, that in the above verse, it has been said 'लोप्येष्वपीष्यते'

The author means to say that if the 'Vivadi' note in a song is very rarely used in a Rāga, then it gets 'Alpatva.' The readers are already advised to use seldom the 'Vivadi' note in a Rāga at its proper place and time.

विवादी विपरीतत्वाद्धीरेरुक्तोरिपूपमः ।
स्वरूपमर्दनं तेन प्रयोगे स्याद्विवादिना ॥
स्वरूपमर्दनाभावे गीते रक्तिनं लभ्यते ।
शत्रूपमर्दने हि स्याद्राज्ञां लोके प्रकाशनम् ॥
नृपामात्यानुसारित्वादनुवादी तु भृत्यवत् ॥

The 'Vivadi' swaras can also be used to alter the cadence of a Rāga and in such a case the notes should be given 'Alpatva.' So far we have dealt with the opinion of ancient authors and the aim was to get the readers acquainted with the manifestations of the Aalap singing of a Rāga. Perhaps the readers now understand that all the distinguishing features of the Aalap singing of a Rāga have been taken from the ancient and medieval literature on music. It has already been mentioned that the 'Jati Gayana' was in vogue before the 'Rāga Gayana' was introduced.

गहाँशतारमंद्राश्चन्यासपम्यासकौतथा   ।
अपिसन्यासविन्यासौ बहुत्वंचाल्पता ततः ॥
एतान्यंतरमार्गेण सह लक्ष्माणि जातिषु ।
षाडबौडुवितेे क्वापीत्येवमाहुस्त्रयोदश   ॥

When 'Jati Gayana' was dropped and 'Rāga Gayana' became current then all these essentials came into use in the 'Rāga Gayana.'

रंजयन्ति मनाँसीति रागास्ते दशलक्षणाः ।
लक्षणानि दशोक्तानि लक्ष्यन्ते तावदादितः ॥

'Rupak—Aalap.'

'Rupak ālap' is another variety of the ancient 'Ālap Gayana,' and so all the characteristics of 'Rāga Ālap' apply to it also. But there is one thing which distinguishes it from other kinds of Ālap.

रूपकं तु तद्वदेव पृथग्भूत विदारिकम् ॥

In 'Rupaka Ālap' the musicians had to demonstrate clearly all the parts of Ālap like the Dhatus of the Prabandhas and the last cadences of such divisions were known as 'Apanyas.' Pt. Kallinath defines the difference between the ancient 'Ālap' and 'Rupak-alap' as follows:

पृथग्भूता विच्छिद्य विच्छिद्य प्रयुक्तविदार्यो गीत खंडानि
यस्मिन्निति । अपन्यासेषु अविरम्य एकाकारेण प्रवृत आलापः ।
स एव अपन्यासेषु विरम्य विरम्य प्रवृत्तं रूपकम् ।

From this it is realised that to the audience of the old days, Rupaka may be the variety of a song—in which words were not at all used. In a Rāga Ālap, musician had to show to the audience what Rāga he was singing, by means of bringing before them all the characteristics that have been dealt with under the caption of Ālap. Rupakalap was like Prabandhas, but it lacked in words and 'Tala' etc. Rupakalap was more extensive than the Rāgalap, in other words, Rupakalap was a step further from Rāgalap.

Ālapti

'Alapti' was an advanced form of Ālap singing. In 'Alapti' singing the Rāga has to be very clearly explained with all the significance. In addition to that, the musician had also to show the 'Avirbhava' and 'Tirobhava' which is clearly explained below.

Avirbhava and Tirobhava.

It is already said that many Rāgas can be derived from a 'Mela' or 'Thata.' While a musician is developing his Rāga by means of different combinations of notes, it is just probable that the audience feel that fragments of Rāgas which are almost similiar to it are combined together. For some combinations of notes of similar Rāgas are bound to occur and they may give to the audience an impression of different Rāgas being combined. A clever musician, however, often places some special or independent passages of his Rāga at a suitable place and thus removes the doubt among the listeners when a Rāga is thus hidden and unidentifiable, the situation is known as 'Tirobhava' and when the Rāga is again manifested it is to be 'Avirbhava.' These 'Bhavas' are very interesting.

Bibliography

BRHADDESI by Matanga Muni. A Sanskrit work on music. Edited by K. Sambasiva Sastri, Curator. The Government Publication Department of Sanskrit Manuscripts, Trivandrum, 1930.

DUTTILAM by Duttilla, the son and also a disciple of Bharat. Edited by the Curator of the Department-for the Publication of Sanskrit Manuscripts, Trivendrum, 1930.

HRIDAYA PRAKASH AND HRIDAYA KAUTUK by Hridaya Narayan Deva, 17th Santury AD, Both these books were kept in the Library of the All India Marir. College of Hindusthani Music, Lucknow till, 1945 (Sanskrit).

LAKSHYA SANGEETAM by Pt. V. N. Bhatkhande, Published by Bhalchandra Sita Ram Sukhthankar, Arya Bhushan Press, Poona City, 1934 (Sanskrit).

NATYA SHASTRA by Bharat. A monumental work on the art of dance and drama in Sanskrit. In which only a few chapters are devoted to music of his time between 4th and 5th century AD. Chaukhambha Sanskrit Series Office, Vidya Vilas Press, Benares, 1929.

RAAG TARANGINI by Lochana Pundit. 16th century AD. The author for the first time ignoring the traditional system of 'grama,' 'murchhana,' and 'jati

gayana,' itroduced the method of 'janya-janak' or
'mela' theory, the same had been adopted by all
scholars of music of later age. Pubished by Bhalchandra Sita Ram Sukhthankar, Arya Bhusan Press,
Poona City, 1918 (Sanskrit).

RAAG TATVA VIBODHA by Srinivas Pundit. 18th
century. The author had rigidly excluded from his
text the medieval system of raag and raagini and
followed the foot steps of his predecessors. His own
contribution to music was the method of locating
the 'swara' on Veena by means of the length of the
wire on scientific basis. Published by Bhalchandra
Sita Ram Sukhthankar at the Arya Bhusan Press,
Poona City 1918 (Sanskrit).

SANGEET DARPANA by Pt. Damodar Mishra. This is
the only book that provides all informations regarding the system of medieval Raag and Raagini, a
very rare book not available at present. There was
only one copy of it in the Library of the Benares
Hindu univrsity till 1930 (Sanskrit).

SANGEET MAKARANDA by Narada. A very rare book
on music in Sanskrit. Not available at present. A
copy of this book was available at the Imperial
Library, Calcutta till 1940.

SANGEET PARIJAT by Pt. Ahovala. This book is also
very rare. There was a copy of it in the personal
library of the late Pt. V.N. Bhatkhande, Malabar
Hill, Bombay till 1936 (Sanskrit).

SANGEET RATNAKAR by Saranga Deva, 13th cetury.
This is the book that should be studied by the post
graduate students and research scholars. Edited by
Mangesh Ram Krishana Telang and Venayak
Ganesh Apte. Published by Ananda Ashram Prin-
ting press, Bombay, 1942 (Sanskrit).

Index

Ahobala 41, 43-45
Anudatya 3, 7
apsarās 2
Ārchika 5
Aroha 45-46, 65
Aryans 2
Ascetic 2
asthaiee 57
Avaroha 45-6, 65
avarohi 57

Bhārat 2
Bhairava 32, 67
Bhairavi 34, 70
Brihadesi 8

Dāmodar 24, 29
Deepaka 37
Dhanasree 36
Dutila 8

Gamaka 46
Gandharvas 2
Gauri 34
Gayana 56
Graha 42
Grāma 7

Hanuman Mata 18
Hridaya Narayana Deva 37

Jati 7

Kafi 69
Kalinath 17
Karnat 35
Kautuka 37
Kedar 35
Khamach 67
Kinnaras 2

Lochana 33, 37

Marva 69
Matanga, Muni 9
Mela 44, 46
Moorchana 7
Mukhari 37

Nād 1
Nārada 2, 33
Nayak 24
Neuter 13
Nyasa *Rāgas* 42

Odava *Rāga* 14

Parijat 41
Prakash 37
Prakriti 2
Puravi 68

Purva 37   Tarangini 37
Putra 8   *Tatva Vivodha* 44
                              Thata 51
rāg- 9, 10, 54   Tivra 65
Ṛg 3   Todi 34, 71
Rāgini 24
Ratnākar 17   .   Udatya 3
Ratnavali 33
                              Vadi 65
Sām 3   Varya-Avarya 45
Sampurna 13   Vernas 57
Sanchari 37   Vidyapati 33
Saranga 36   vikrita 7, 50
Sarasvati 5   Vivadi 65
Shadava 14   Vilabal 66
Shiva 2
siksha 20   Yaman 36, 65
Someshwar 30